Routledge Revivals

Holy Images

First published in 1940, this title presents four of the Gifford Lectures in natural theology given by Edwyn Bevan in 1933: 'An Inquiry into Idolatry and Image-Worship in Ancient Paganism and Christianity'. Reference is made throughout all four lectures not only to the conventional disputes in Western Christianity, but also to the attitudes of Hebrew, Pagan, Patristic, Muslim and Eastern thinkers towards the role of symbols and symbolism in worship. In this way, a subject of perennial fascination and importance is placed in a broad historical context, and innovative lines of enquiry are developed with clarity and insight.

Holy Images offers an intriguing and accessible resource to students of theology, comparative religion, religious anthropology and philosophy.

Holy Images

An Inquiry into Idolatry and Image-Worship in
Ancient Paganism and in Christianity

Edwyn Bevan

First published in 1940
by George Allen & Unwin Ltd

This edition first published in 2014 by Routledge
2 Park Square, Milton Park, Abingdon, Oxon, OX14 4RN

and by Routledge
711 Third Avenue, New York, NY 10017

Routledge is an imprint of the Taylor & Francis Group, an informa business

© 1940 George Allen & Unwin Ltd

All rights reserved. No part of this book may be reprinted or reproduced or utilised in any form or by any electronic, mechanical, or other means, now known or hereafter invented, including photocopying and recording, or in any information storage or retrieval system, without permission in writing from the publishers.

Publisher's Note
The publisher has gone to great lengths to ensure the quality of this reprint but points out that some imperfections in the original copies may be apparent.

Disclaimer
The publisher has made every effort to trace copyright holders and welcomes correspondence from those they have been unable to contact.

A Library of Congress record exists under LC control number: 40014850

ISBN 13: 978-1-138-02378-9 (hbk)
ISBN 13: 978-1-315-77461-9 (ebk)
ISBN 13: 978-1-138-02601-8 (pbk)

HOLY IMAGES

An Inquiry into
Idolatry and Image-Worship
in Ancient Paganism
and in
Christianity

by

EDWYN BEVAN

London
George Allen & Unwin Ltd

FIRST PUBLISHED IN 1940

ALL RIGHTS RESERVED
PRINTED IN GREAT BRITAIN
in 12-Point Fournier Type
BY UNWIN BROTHERS LIMITED
WOKING

PREFACE

THE four lectures which appear, expanded with a good deal of additional matter, in this book were delivered in Edinburgh, on Lord Gifford's Foundation, in 1933. They were not included in the volume which contained the other sixteen lectures (*Symbolism and Belief*), since they constituted a digression on a particular instance of symbolism—the use of carved and painted images in religion—and might be left out without the general argument of that book being affected. It thus seemed to me advisable to make of them a smaller separate volume. They do not deal with such fundamental questions in the philosophy of religious belief as were raised in the larger book, yet a study of image-worship in the ancient world, and, later on, in the Christian Church, does offer many points of peculiar interest—more perhaps that is curious and surprising than anyone unacquainted with the subject might suppose. Nor are the questions it raises all of merely academic interest; some are still controversial questions of vital consequence, both in the Christian Church at home and in the present-day contact between Christian missions and the traditional idolatry of some non-Christian peoples.

I owe special acknowledgment for the valuable help which I received, concerning the Jewish attitude to images in Rabbinical and modern times, from Professor Herbert Loewe, whose large erudition in this field gives me an assurance that this book takes note of what is here mainly important. I also owe thanks to Professor

Holy Images

F. Dvornik, a scholar belonging himself to the Roman Church, but one of our chief authorities on Byzantine ecclesiastical history, and, through him, to Professor George Ostrogorsky for giving me light on some points regarding which I was not clear.

I have also to thank the Gallery of Fine Arts, Yale University, for enabling me to insert a plate showing one of the figures from the frescoes in the ancient Jewish Synagogue at Dura in Mesopotamia (plate i), and the British Museum for supplying photographs of the ivory representing the Crucifixion (plate ii) and the Buddhist bas-relief from the Amravati sculptures (plate iv).

April 1939.

CONTENTS

	PAGE
PREFACE	7
LECTURE I	13
LECTURE II	46
LECTURE III	84
LECTURE IV	113
INDEX	179

LIST OF ILLUSTRATIONS

PLATE FACING PAGE

I FIGURE FROM THE DURA FRESCOES 58
   (Abraham?)

II CRUCIFIXION ON IVORY BOX IN
    THE BRITISH MUSEUM 98

III STATUE OF THE GOOD SHEPHERD
     IN THE LATERAN 100

IV SCENE FROM THE LIFE OF THE
    BUDDHA IN THE AMRAVATI SCULP-
    TURES 102

LECTURE I

Any discussion of symbolism in connexion with religion must make it plain that, whereas, on the one side, religion cannot dispense with symbols for its apprehension and expression, there is, on the other side, a constant liability for the mind to catch in the accidents of the symbol and so confuse, instead of furthering, its approach to reality. There is no kind of symbol in regard to which this liability may seem to be more signally exhibited than the pictorial or plastic images which have been so conspicuous an element in the worship of nearly all religions. These four lectures are devoted to the question of image-worship and idolatry.

By an image we ordinarily mean a visible symbol which represents something else in virtue of formal resemblance. But a material object identified with a god need not resemble anything else: it need not even have any human or animal shape: it may be a shapeless stone or a tree. A portable material object, without human or animal shape, believed to have divine or demonic quality, to be charged with uncanny power, we commonly speak of as a *fetish*, and no hard and fast line can be drawn between such idolatry as identifies the image with the god and fetish-worship. Anthropologists have told us that image-worship was preceded by an earlier stage in which the material objects treated with religious regard by man were *aniconic*, rocks and trees, springs and rivers, not things shaped by men's hands to resemble any living thing. A particular stone, for instance, was believed to possess a

Holy Images

power for good and evil, and it was treated in a way which, it was hoped, would make the power friendly—by smearing things upon it, and so on.

No doubt, it would be a mistake to try to construe the thoughts of primitive man, as if they had the sharp logical definiteness we expect of men's thoughts on the civilized level. They must have been largely vague in outline, wavering and inconsistent, like our thoughts in dreaming, or like the thoughts of children. It would perhaps be impossible to say precisely to what extent primitive man regarded a stone so tended as a person, to what extent just as a thing charged with a peculiar numinous power, a power of good luck or bad luck, like the kind of power for bad luck which some people fear to-day if they walk under a ladder. They do not think of such a power as a malignant person, rather as like a dangerous natural force.

It may be a mistake to think that all objects of worship were aniconic even in the most primitive stages of mankind to which inquiry can reach. Anthropologists believe that the drawings of animals in caves by men of the Early Stone Age had magical significance, because it was supposed that the picture of an animal gave men power over living animals of that species. If so, men at that far-back stage had already come to believe that you can affect living creatures by something you do to objects made to resemble them, and if this held good in the case of animals it would be consonant to believe that you could affect a supernatural being of whom man had an imaginative conception through an object made to resemble him. Thus, it seems likely that aniconic fetishism and a cult of iconic objects existed side by side in Palaeolithic times.

Some aniconic objects continued, because they had

Aniconic Objects of Worship

attached to them the associations of an immemorial tradition, to receive worship in the Graeco-Roman world through the most advanced phases of the ancient civilization. Certain unshaped stones by the wayside still in the last times before the victory of Christianity were anointed and garlanded by pious pagans as having in them some divine power.[1] The most ancient and revered representation of Eros at Thespiae, close to the image of the god by Praxiteles, Greek art in its perfection, was a rude block of stone.[2] At Lindos in Rhodes, Athena was represented by a smooth board, and Hera in Samos by a rough one, "because so in those old days did men set up gods."[3] At Sparta, the Dioscuri were represented by two parallel upright pieces of wood.[4] At Pharae in Achaia, close to the image of Hermes, "there stand," Pausanias writes, "about thirty square stones: these the people of Pharae revere, giving to each stone the name of a god. In the olden time all the Greeks worshipped unwrought stones instead of images."[5]

We can understand how the worship of unwrought stones may have led in many cases to the worship of graven images. One reason why a particular stone was sometimes chosen for worship was that it bore an accidental resemblance to a living form. If so, the resemblance

---
[1] Lucian, *Alexander*, 30; Arnobius, *Adv. Nat.*, i. 39.
[2] Pausanias, ix. 27. 1.
[3] Οὔπω Σκέλμιον ἔργον εὔξοον, ἀλλ' ἔτι τεθμῷ
δηναίῳ γλυφάνων ἄξοος ἦσθα σάνις·
ὧδε γὰρ ἱδρύοντο θεοὺς τότε· καὶ γὰρ Ἀθήνης
ἐν Λίνδῳ Δαναὸς λεῖον ἔθηκεν ἕδος.
Callimachus, quoted in Eusebius, *Praep. Evang.* iii. 8.
[4] Plutarch, *De frat. amore*. 1.
[5] Pausanias, vii. 22. 4. In his note on this passage, Sir James Frazer gives a large number of instances amongst other peoples of the worship of unwrought stones.

Holy Images

might be increased by a few rude modifications made by the hand of man, signs cut or scratched upon the stone to represent eyes or mouth or other organs. A gradual process would lead from such rude beginnings to the carving, by perfected art, of an image in human form. When the Greeks reached the level of higher civilization, all the new representations of divine beings were graven or molten images in the likeness of man. The aniconic objects still worshipped were very old, things surviving from a stage of culture left far behind. It was only because they were so old that a numinous awe attached to them. So far as a spirit or demon had been thought of in those old days as inhabiting an unwrought natural object, the object had not been taken to show what the spirit itself looked like, except in those cases where it had been chosen for worship because its shape accidentally suggested a human form. The stone was the habitation, not the portrait, of the spirit. But in the days of Phidias and Praxiteles, the Greeks did think that their gods, if manifested to the eyes of man, looked like that. The images now were held not only to be a means of communication with the gods, but to give information about them. We have now image-worship in the full sense—the image-worship which some great religions have sternly condemned as a deadly aberration—Judaism, Zoroastrianism, Islam, some forms of Christianity, some forms of modern Hinduism.

Here we have to notice that the condemnation of image-worship has been based upon different grounds—grounds which would be incompatible with each other if referred to one conception of image-worship only, but which may have their justification if the different grounds given are taken as applying, one ground to one con-

Idolatry as Pure Delusion

cept of image-worship, and another ground to another conception.

One view is that there is no reality at all corresponding with the image: behind the image is mere blank and emptiness. That must, of course, be the view taken by Rationalists or Materialists. Idolatry, so looked at, cannot be considered anything wicked, but simply as a pitiable and harmful absurdity, an utter waste of time and effort and emotion. And a great deal of the denunciation of idolatry from the religious side also has proceeded on the supposition that it is pure delusion, so far as the gods of polytheism go: there is no reality at all corresponding with the idea of Marduk or Osiris or Apollo or Vishnu: "The heathen in his blindness bows down to wood and stone." Yet so far as idolatry appears, not only as foolish but as wicked—and from the religious side it has always been denounced as wicked—that can only be because the denunciation presupposes the real existence of a spiritual world, with which men, in worshipping the idol, are seeking to come into contact, and seeking in the wrong way.

The attack on idolatry in the Old Testament is on two lines according as it is pagan idolatry, the worship of false gods, or the worship of the true God, of Jehovah, by means of images, which is attacked. We must keep the two apart. In regard to the worship of pagan gods, the Old Testament usually speaks as if there were no reality at all corresponding with them, as if they were mere air, vanity, false imagination. It takes, that is to say, the same view which might be taken by a Rationalist, except that it believes in the existence all the time of the one true God to whom men ought to turn in worship, instead of to dumb idols, and therefore believes idolatry to be

Holy Images

wicked. If the idol is simply inanimate matter and nothing more, then all the tendance of it by man can be exhibited as pure absurdity.

"The idols of the nations are silver and gold, the work of men's hands. They have mouths but they speak not; eyes have they, but they see not; they have ears, but they hear not; neither is there any breath in their mouths." (Psalm cxxxv. 15, 16.)

Or the author of Isaiah xliv:

"Who hath fashioned a god, or molten an idol that is profitable for nothing? . . . The carpenter stretcheth out a line; he marketh it out with a pencil; he shapeth it with planes, and he marketh it out with the compasses, and shapeth it after the figure of a man, to dwell in the house. He . . . strengtheneth for himself one among the trees of the forest; he planteth a fir-tree and the rain doth nourish it. . . . He burneth part thereof in the fire; with part thereof he eateth flesh; he roasteth roast and is satisfied; yea, he warmeth himself and saith, Aha, I am warm, I have seen the fire; and the residue thereof he maketh a god. . . . He falleth down to it and worshippeth, and prayeth unto it and saith, Deliver me; for thou art my god."

The same motive is worked out with further imaginative details in the Book of Wisdom—the choice of a tree by the woodcutter, the burning of part of it to cook food, the use of the remainder to make an image, the painting and fixing of the image in a shrine, and then the prayer offered to the lifeless thing.

"He is not ashamed to speak to that which hath no life:
Yea for health he calleth upon that which is weak,
And for life he beseecheth that which is dead,
And for aid he supplicateth that which hath least experience,

Old Testament Denunciation

And for a good journey that which cannot so much as move a step,
And for gaining and getting and good success of his hands He asketh ability of that which with its hands is most unable."

(Wisdom xiii. 10–19.)

Or take the Epistle of Jeremy, the Hebrew original of which is thought to belong to a date soon after the Greek conquest of the East:

"Gods of silver and of gold and of wood, borne upon shoulders, which cause the nations to fear. . . . Their tongue is polished by the workman, and they themselves are overlaid with gold and with silver; yet are they but false and cannot speak. And taking gold, as it were for a virgin that loveth to go gay, men make crowns for the heads of their gods. . . . Yet cannot these gods save themselves from rust and moths, though they be covered with purple raiment. Men wipe their faces because of the dust of the temple which is thick upon them. . . . They are as one of the beams of the temple; and men say that their hearts are eaten out, when things creeping out of the earth devour both them and their raiment: they feel it not when their faces are blackened through the smoke that cometh out of the temple: upon their bodies and heads alight bats, swallows and other birds; and in like manner cats also." (Baruch vi. 4–22.)

And so on, for the chapter is a long one, and the mockery is spun out in a way which is apt to appear tedious; for if people really believe that an image is a god when it is only wood or stone, the absurdity is so obvious that to go on exhibiting this in one point of detail after another may be felt as too facile an exercise of wit.

But can the nations surrounding the Israelites—

Holy Images

Egyptians, Syrians, Babylonians, Greeks—have been fairly charged with an absurdity so patent as to imagine that the image which they knew to have been shaped by human hands was really alive?

It is hardly possible that anyone thought of the deity worshipped as simply the image he saw and nothing more. The personality of the deity was not confined to the image in the sense in which my personality is confined to my body. The deity was certainly conceived of as a person active in the world apart from the image. No Samian in historical times can ever have supposed that the sacred board, even if in some way it was animated by Hera, was all there was of Hera. The most primitive-minded Samian no doubt imagined Hera as a being in human form, a glorified woman with her regal throne in some unseen abode of the gods. Hera had many different images in different places, and if she in some way animated them all, she herself was not any one of them. We are told indeed that in Italy within the last century the peasantry has sometimes so deified their own particular local Madonna that the partisans of one Madonna would fight for her honour against those of another Madonna. But it may be questioned whether, even in such a case, any Italian peasant thinks that the Mother of God is sheerly identical with her local image, and that the neighbouring Madonna is another person. If any peasant were pressed to explain his beliefs, he would probably say that the Mother of God who lives in heaven works miracles on the earth through her images, and that his local image is a more favoured instrument for the Madonna than the Madonna of another district. So far as he feels hostility to the other Madonna it would really be hostility to the people of the other place who say that their image is as

The Image and the Deity

good a one as his, and he would hate the sight of the other Madonna only in so far as it is the mascot of the rival village. It may be that educated observers who describe primitive survivals in present-day custom are inclined rather to overstate the amount of such belief which goes with them, making them in that way more telling and curious as instances which illustrate an anthropological theory. I do not know that there is any evidence of an ancient Greek regarding one Athena or Apollo as a distinct person from another Athena or Apollo, apart from mere comic mockery, as in Lucian's *Zeus Tragoedus*, where the bronze Hermes of the agora is brought in as a different person from the Hermes who acts as divine messenger in heaven: they are called brothers.

To the Greeks and Romans of the days when the ancient culture was at its highest, the actual identification of an image with a god was an idea which could only be entertained by the educated as a jest. The passage of Horace comes to mind:

> "Once I was a fig-tree, good-for-nothing wood, when the craftsman, after hesitating a while whether to make me a stool or a Priapus, decided for the god." (*Satires*, I. 8, 1.)

It is a striking parallel to the passage of Isaiah, quoted just now, where the craftsman uses part of his log for fuel, and part to make a god of; only, whereas the Hebrew prophet speaks in burning indignation, the Roman poet is, of course, only making play with an absurdity. The absurdity is elsewhere used for jesting. Dionysius the younger of Syracuse stripped an image of Zeus of its mantle of gold and replaced it by a woollen one, remarking that the god would find the woollen one both lighter and

Holy Images

warmer in winter.[1] Lucilius speaks of the idea that bronze statues are alive as a fancy of small children.[2] Plutarch in one passage inveighs against the common mode of speech by which the image is identified with the god. "Amongst the Greeks," he says, "there were those who beheld representations of the gods in bronze or in stone or in painting and, through lack of knowledge and education, fell to calling such images 'gods,' instead of saying 'images' or 'symbols' of the gods. One might hear men say that Lachares had robbed Athena, or that Dionysius had cut off the golden curls of Apollo, or that Jupiter of the Capitol had been burnt in the days of the Civil War. Men fail to observe that such incorrect ways of speaking lead actually to false notions."[3] The story of Stilpo has sometimes been adduced to prove the opposite, that the Greeks in the fourth century B.C. did actually identify the images with the gods. But the story really tells the other way. Stilpo, we are told, in sophist wise, entrapped a disputant by asking first:

"Athena is the daughter of Zeus, is she not?"

"Yes."

"But this Athena (pointing to the image) was not produced by Zeus but by Phidias?"

His opponent agrees.

"Then," Stilpo concludes, "Athena is not a goddess."[4]

He was condemned because the conclusion had an ill sound, and was, of course, intended to shock: but the

[1] Clement of Alexandria, *Protrept.*, iv. § 46.

[2] Ut pueri infantes credunt signa omnia aena
Vivere et esse homines, sic isti somnia ficta
Vera putant; credunt signis cor inesse in aenis.
Pergula pictorum veri nihil omnia ficta.
Lucilius, *Reliquiae*, lines 486–8.

[3] *Isis and Osiris*, 71.   [4] Diogenes Laertius, ii. 11, § 116.

Egyptian Tendance of Images

opponent, notice, agrees as a matter of course, when Stilpo points to the image and says: "This Athena is not of Zeus, but of Phidias?"

Yet it is quite plain that these peoples did think of the god as in some sense animating the image—animating all the many consecrated images there might be of him in different places. The image was not the one body of the god, but it was his body in so far as what you did to the image—hanging it with garlands, washing it, making music and burning sacrifice before it—was pleasurably felt by the god, and the god on the other hand could put forth his power or declare his mind through the image. For Egypt, we have detailed information about the daily ritual at certain temples. "At Abydos," Erman tells us, "the priest first offered incense in the hypostyle hall, saying: 'I come into thy presence, O Great One, after I have purified myself. . . . I come to do what ought to be done, but I do not come to do what ought not to be done.' He then stepped in front of the shrine of the god and opened the seal of clay with these words: 'The clay is broken and the seal loosed that this door may be opened, and all that is evil in me I throw on the ground.' " Next, after incensing the sacred cobra and greeting it by its names, he approached with prescribed ritual words the part of the temple where the idol stood. "The toilet of the god then commenced. He 'laid his hands on him,' took off the old rouge and his former clothes, all of course with the necessary formulas. He then dressed the god in the robe called the *nems*, saying: 'Come, white dress! come, white dress! Come, white eye of Horus, which proceedeth from the town of Nechebt. The gods dress themselves with thee in thy name *Dress*, the gods adorn themselves with thee in thy name *Adornment*.'

Holy Images

The priest then dressed the god in the *great dress*, rouged him and presented him with his insignia—the sceptre, the ruler's staff, the whip, the bracelets and anklets, as well as the two feathers he wore on his head, because he 'has triumphed over his enemies, and is more splendid than gods or spirits'. . . . Not only had the priest to dress and serve his god, but he had also to feed him; food and drink had to be placed daily on the table of offerings, and on festival days extra gifts were due." Beside the daily ritual, there were the occasions when an idol was taken out of the temple and carried in procession in his sacred boat, so strictly enclosed, it would seem, that the eyes of the worshipping people saw only the boat, but not the image itself.[1]

Amongst the Greeks it is not likely that the tendance of the images was as elaborate as in Egypt, though analogous ceremonies were everywhere customary. There are numerous notices of images being dressed in beautiful clothes, being perfumed, and crowned with garlands. It was common for images to be given, once a year, a ritual washing. The fifth of the Hymns of Callimachus purports to be an address to the maidens who wait upon the image of Pallas at Argos on the occasion of the goddess's bath.

The image served not only as a means by which men could honour and please the god, but as a means by which the god could bestow benefits on men. The tract entitled *Asklepios*, belonging to the Greek Hermetic literature produced in Egypt, itself a late document, put by W. Scott between A.D. 260 and 310, but embodying ideas which had come down in the religious tradition of Egypt, speaks of "statues living and conscious, filled with

[1] *Life in Ancient Egypt*, English translation by H. M. Tirard, Macmillan, 1894, p. 274.

The Image as Alive

the breath of life, and doing many mighty works; statues which have foreknowledge, and predict future events by the drawing of lots, and by prophetic inspiration, and by dreams, and in many other ways, statues which inflict diseases and heal them, dispensing sorrow and joy according to men's deserts." In connexion with Alexander the Great's visit to the Oasis of Siwa, one Greek account says that the image of Amen-Re gave oracles by making particular movements. Maspero believed that it was a case of what *we* might consider fraud, though the procedure, he supposes, was well-known and was not considered fraudulent by the people of the time. "Like all prophetic images," Maspero wrote, "this one too was constructed so as to be able to make a limited number of gestures, move its head, wave its arms or hands. A priest pulled the string."[1]

As for Greek religion, there are a good many stories in classical literature narrating how some particular image gave a sign of the god's mind or of some impending event. The image of Hera at Sybaris was said to have turned on its pedestal while a stream of blood welled up from the ground, to express the goddess's wrath at the evil deeds of the Sybarites.[2] Dio Cassius says that on the day of the battle of Pharsalos, the image of goddess Nike (Victory) in the temple at Tralles turned towards the image of Julius Caesar in the same temple.[3] The image of Athena Parthenos at Athens, Dio Cassius says, in the year 21 B.C. turned round from its eastward position towards the west and spat blood.[4] At the time of the war between Rome and Aristonicus, the son of the last king of Pergamon (130–129 B.C.), a legend recorded by

[1] *Etudes de mythologie et d'archéologie égyptiennes*, vi. (1912), p. 271.
[2] Athenaeus, xii. 521 f.   [3] Book xli. 61.   [4] Book liv. 7.

Holy Images

St. Augustine stated that the image of Apollo at Cumae in Asia Minor shed tears for the space of four days.[1]

More stories of the same kind may be found in Charly Clerc's book[2] (pp. 45-9), but they cannot be pressed to show a belief in the actual animation of the image, because stories of similar portents are told in connexion with the statues of living men. A stone statue of Mark Antony, near Alba, for instance, went on perspiring, Plutarch says, for several days, when war between him and Octavian became imminent, in spite of its being continually wiped.[3] The statue of the Sicilian tyrant Hiero at Delphi fell from its pedestal on the day of Hiero's death (467 B.C.).[4] The portent, therefore, in the case of the images of gods, might be regarded rather as the use of the material image by the Divine Power to give a sign than as an action done by the image. There seems something more like belief in a virtue residing in the image itself, when men receive benefits by looking at an image, or touching it. There are a number of such cases asserted in the Greek books. Charly Clerc has, however, observed that they all refer to images, not of the great gods, but of semi-deified men or heroes. It was such intermediate beings who must have been felt as nearer to men, more apt to act as helpers and healers. There is the image of Hector at Ilion, which, Philostratus says, "is so much alive that it draws on the beholder to touch it. It bestows much good both on societies and

---

[1] *De Civit. Dei*, iii. 11. Augustine, by an obvious inadvertence, calls it a war "adversus *Achaeos* regemque Aristonicum." Charly Clerc makes the confusion worse by translating this "la guerre des Achéens contre le roi Aristonicos."

[2] *Les Théories relatives au Culte des Images chez les auteurs grecs du iime siècle après J.-C.* (Fontemoing & Co., Paris, 1915).

[3] *Anton.*, 60. [4] *De Pyth. Orac.*, 8.

Virtue Residing in Images

on individuals, for which reason prayer is offered to it."[1] The image of Protesilaus in the Thracian Chersonese had been largely worn away by the anointing and handling of worshippers.[2] At Athens there was a stele which had a bas-relief of the Scythian physician Toxaris: cases were alleged in which persons suffering from fever had been cured by it.[3] Lucian refers to a similar belief about the statue of the athlete Polydamas at Olympia; this also had the virtue of curing fevers.[4] It was especially the athlete Theagenes of Thasos, whose statues were believed to heal diseases. The original statue was in his native Thasos, but in many places of the Greek world and even amongst the barbarians, Pausanias says, statues of Theagenes were erected and tended, and they proved to have healing power.[5]

If we ask how men could imagine an image made by human hands to be connected in this way with an unseen person, it has to be remembered that such a view of images was part of the whole way of thinking about the universe implied in what anthropologists to-day call "sympathetic magic." If it were true that you could destroy your enemy by melting a little wax image of him in the fire, or cause him to suffer pain by running nails into such an image, it was quite consonant to suppose that you make a god hear by talking to his image, or please him by decorating it. Psychologically, no doubt, such beliefs were not calm inferences of reason from the observed connexion between phenomena, but understandable as the outcome of intense desire and passion. If your hatred of your enemy had reached a point when

[1] *Heroïc.*, ii. 10, p. 151, Kayser.
[2] Philostr. *Heroïc.*, ii. 1, p. 141, Kayser.
[3] Lucian, *Scyth.*, 2.   [4] *Deorum Concilium*, 12.   [5] vi. 11. 9.

Holy Images

it must discharge itself in some action, and your enemy was at a distance, out of your reach, it was a relief to vent your hatred upon the little image, and as you ran the nail into its eye you could not help feeling, by the relief you experienced, that your enemy was feeling something unpleasant. Just so, if you had an urgent desire to make the divine helper hear your cry of distress, and the divine helper was invisible, seemingly beyond the reach of your voice, it was a relief to pour your prayer into the stone ear of the idol: by that same law of the universe which worked in the case of the waxen image, you got confidence that the unseen deity heard.

In the *Seven against Thebes* of Aeschylus, the maidens who are terrified lest the protecting gods forsake the city assailed by an alien army, cling to the feet of the ancient idols—ἀκμάζει βρετέων ἔχεσθαι. They are quite aware that the idols are not identical with the deities prayed to. It is a horrible possibility that the deities may go away to another land; the maidens reason with them, urging that they will nowhere be able to find a more desirable home than Thebes, ποῖον δ' ἀμείψεσθε γαίας πέδον τᾶσδ' ἄρειον; they know that the idols anyway will stand where they do now. Yet the maidens feel that by holding the idols' feet, they are in some way preventing the gods from going away.

There are a number of cases mentioned in which images were actually chained: one was at Tyre before Alexander took the city: an image of Apollo was chained to the altar of Melkarth.[1] Sir J. Frazer in a note on Pausanias,[2] gives parallels from all over the world. In Isaiah the pagan Babylonians are represented as chaining their idols under terror of the Persian attack.[3] At Athens,

---
[1] Curt. Ruf., iv. 3. § 15.   [2] iii. 15. 7.   [3] xl. 19.

Idolatry as Sympathetic Magic

at the festival of the Skirophoria, when it was urgent to bring home to the gods the land's need of rain, an image of Athena was perhaps rubbed with dry, caked earth.[1] Many anthropologists believe that the custom of bathing the images was not originally a mere attention in which their toilet was assimilated to that of a man, but an outcome of ancient rain-magic, performed with the same object as the Athenian smearing with dust, though in one case what was desired and in the other what was dreaded was applied to the image. This kind of feeling in regard to the images of the gods must have been general. It would probably be impossible to say precisely what theory it implied—in most cases, we may be sure, no rationalized, articulate theory of the connexion between the idol and the god—only a feeling that somehow the god felt what you did to the idol.

Between the belief of the peasant, who took the animation of the idol in its most gross realistic sense, and the belief of the educated man, who regarded the ceremonies

[1] There was a temple of Athena Skīras in the Ceramicus and another at Phalerum. The festival, *Skīra*, took place in the hot time of the year, and one explanation of the name given in antiquity was that it was called after the parasols (*skīra*) carried ceremonially at the festival. There is, however, a word *skīros* or *skirros* which means "gypsum," "stucco," and *gē skirras*, the Scholiast on Aristophanes, *Wasps*, 925, says, means "white earth like gypsus." So another explanation of the surname of this Athena was that it should be pronounced *skirras* and that it was given to her because she was smeared ceremonially "with white." The Scholiast does not definitely say that this "white" was *gē skirras*, or that the smearing, if it occurred, took place at the festival of Skira. Modern scholars have conjectured that the Scholiast, or his source, knew of some ceremony of smearing Athena Skiras with dry earth, which really took place, as a relic of rain magic, and that he therefore hit on the guess that her surname was connected with a word for white-caked earth, though the etymological connexion of *skiras* with *skirros* or *skiros* is rather a questionable supposition.

Holy Images

of worship as only expressing in a symbolic way that there was some unseen power somewhere, who liked to receive the homage of men, there may have been any number of intermediate shades. And the accessibility of the idol was far from always giving complete assurance that access was secured to the deity. In the beginning of the third century B.C., a time when rationalism had eaten far into ancient beliefs, the Athenians in their hymn to the Macedonian prince Demetrius contrast him with the far-away gods, whom men could only apprehend by means of idols.

> "God mighty and near!
> The other gods are far away somewhere,
>   Or cannot hear,
> Or are not, or for men have no concern:
>   Thy form we see,
> A living god, not wood or stone, and turn
>   Dear god, to Thee." [1]

Had a man like Horace, we may ask, no belief at all in the reality of a goddess corresponding with the idea of Venus, when he promised Venus, on certain conditions, a new image in a beautiful temple?

> "By the Alban lake that day
> 'Neath citron roof all marble shalt thou stand:
> Incense there and fragrant spice
> With odorous fumes thy nostrils shall salute;
> Blended notes thine ears entice,
> The lyre, the pipe, the Berecyntine flute:
> Graceful youths and maidens bright
> Shall twice a day thy tuneful praise resound,
> While their feet, so fair and white,
> In Salian measure three times beat the ground." [2]

---

[1] Athenaeus, vi. 253 e.
[2] Odes, iv. 1. 19–29. (Conington's translation.)

Ritual to Make the Image Alive

If one had questioned Horace about his view of the universe, he would no doubt have given an account of it, according to his articulate professed intellectual belief on rationalist Epicurean lines, which made it absurd to suppose any real connexion between a marble image and a goddess. But we realize more to-day than was realized before how the mind of man is on various levels, and how, beneath an articulate intellectual theory, a belief inconsistent with that theory, closely connected with unavowed feelings and desires, may still subsist. Certainly, the great majority of people in Horace's day believed that the ritual offered before the images gave pleasure to real personal powers, and we may well doubt whether a poet to whom the idea of the beautiful temple, the lovely marble image, the white feet of the youths and the maidens, the incense and the music, was aesthetically attractive, was quite sure that it was all mere play-acting.

But it was widely believed that simply to make an image of the god was not enough to establish the close sympathetic connexion between the image and the god; you had to do something more. The image, as it left the hands of the craftsman, was just wood or stone; but by the proper rites you could induce the deity to animate it, to make it an organ for his reception of your worship and his bestowal of help. This is the established practice in Hinduism to-day. Before its ritual animation, the image is not a fit object of worship: afterwards it really becomes one of the visible bodies of the god. The consecration includes the recitation by the Brahmin priest of particular ritual verses, rubbing particular substances upon the outside of the image, and, in some districts, putting sacred objects of some kind inside it.[1]

[1] W. Crooke in Hastings' *Encycl. of Religion and Ethics*, vii. pp. 144, 145.

Holy Images

A similar practice is found among more primitive peoples.

"Among the Negroes of the West Coast there are regular shops for fetishes and idols, kept by sorcerers. The purchaser makes his choice, and it is only then that the sorcerer causes the spirit to descend into the idol. Among the New Zealanders, the priest makes the souls of the dead pass into statues which he shakes up and down as if he were rousing a sleeping man."[1]

So far as I know, there is no clear evidence of such a practice amongst the ancient Greeks. Certain ceremonies of consecration took place indeed when an image was set up. A Scholiast on Aristophanes tells us that it was the custom to offer bowls of porridge on such an occasion to the deity represented.[2] A writer (Anticlides) quoted by Athenaeus, describes the offering of a mixture of certain liquids in an urn when the image was one of Zeus Ktēsios.[3] And other writers in the later days of paganism imply that the ceremony of consecration made the image somehow different from what it was before. In the dialogue written by Minucius Felix, the Christian disputant is made to ask with mordant sarcasm: "When does this god come into being? The image is molten, hammered or carved. It is not yet a god. Next it is soldered, pieced

[1] Count G. d'Alviella in Hastings' *Encycl. of Religion and Ethics*, vii. p. 113.

[2] Ἔθος γὰρ ἦν ἐν ταῖς ἱδρύσεσι τῶν ἀγαλμάτων ὀσπρίων ἡψημένων χύτρας περιπομπεύεσθαι ὑπὸ γυναικῶν ποικίλως ἡμφιεσμένων· καὶ τούτων ἀπήρχοντο, χαριστήρια τοῖς θεοῖς ἀπονέμοντες. Schol. to Aristophanes, *Plutus*, 1197. The Scholium in the Codex Dorvillianus says: Ἀφιεροῦντές τι ἐν ναοῖς ἢ καθιδρύοντες αὐτοὺς ἔθος εἶχον προσάγειν χύτρας ἀθάρας καὶ σεμιδάλεως μέστας ἢ πελάνων καὶ ὀσπρίων ἀληλεσμένων.

For further references see G. Wolff, *Porphyrii de Philosophia ex Oraculis haurienda reliquiae* (Berlin, 1856), pp. 206–13.

[3] Athen., xi. 473 c.

Greek and Roman Consecration

together, set up on its base. No, it is not a god yet. Then it is decorated, consecrated, prayed to. Ah, now at last it is a god, when man has so willed and performed the consecration."[1] But this passage, perhaps, could hardly be pressed to show that a particular ceremony was believed to have the effect which the ceremony of consecration is believed to have in India. Minucius may be simply making a rhetorical contrast between the image in the workshop of the maker and the image later on as an object of worship in the temple. But other notices show that the ceremony of consecration was believed, in the later times at any rate, of paganism, to make a difference. Plutarch, in his life of Coriolanus, mentions a legend that an image of Fortuna Muliebris put up by the mother and wife of Coriolanus, was heard to speak, and Dionysius of Halicarnassus said that this occurred "on the first day of its consecration."[2]

There is an odd story in Dio Cassius[3] that when in 142 B.C., Mummius, the conqueror of Corinth, lent some valuable images, apparently unconsecrated ones, to Lucullus for the temporary adornment of a new temple on the occasion of its consecration, Lucullus afterwards refused to give them back, on the ground that by being in the temple during the ceremony of consecration the images in question had become consecrated too.

Some kind of holiness was thus believed by Greeks and Romans to attach to images after consecration, though this might not amount to actual animation, such as Hinduism supposes. But an idea closely parallel to the Indian idea was evidently entertained in Hellenistic Egypt. In the Hermetic tract, *Asklepios*, just referred to,

[1] *Octavius*, 23.   [2] *Antiqu. Rom.*, viii. 56.   [3] xxii. frag. 76.

Holy Images

we get it frankly expounded, and the writer glories in the fact that men can make gods.

"They invented," we are told, "the art of making gods out of some material substance; that it to say, being unable to make souls, they invoked the souls of daemons, and implanted them in the statues by means of certain holy and sacred rites." Such terrestrial gods, the tract goes on to say, are particularly touchy: they "are easily provoked to anger, inasmuch as they are made and put together by men out of both kinds of substance." The other interlocutor in the dialogue asks for further information regarding the means by which the daemons are induced to come and reside in the images, and he gets the answer: "They are induced by herbs and stones and scents which have in them something divine. And would you know why frequent sacrifices are offered to do them pleasure, with hymns and praises and concord of sweet sounds that imitate heaven's harmony? These things are done to the end that, gladdened by oft-repeated worship, the heavenly beings who have been enticed into the images may continue through long ages to acquiesce in the companionship of men. Thus it is that man makes gods."[1]

Suidas has preserved a fragment of Damascius which tells us of an Alexandrine philosopher, Heraïskos (latter part of fifth century A.D.), who "had a natural gift of discernment in regard to sacred images, whether they were alive or not. The moment he looked at one, if it was alive, he felt a stab of peculiar feeling go through his heart: his soul and body were both agitated, as if he were divinely possessed. If, on the other hand, he felt no such emotion, the image was a lifeless one, destitute of

[1] Translation of W. Scott. *Hermetica*, vol. 1, p. 359.

Animated Images

any divine spirit. It was in this way that he knew, by what may be truly called a mystical union with the deity, that the awful image of Aion was inhabited by the god whom the Alexandrines worshipped, and who is Osiris and Adonis in one."[1]

In view of these testimonies we may ask whether the mockery of the old Hebrew books is not justified, when it ridicules the absurdity of supposing images of wood and stone to be living beings? So far as conceptions such as the Indian and Egyptian ones just spoken of have prevailed, we can hardly deny that the charge brought by the Hebrews against idolaters is substantiated. One may sometimes to-day hear superior persons rebuke the stupid narrow-mindedness of European Christians, especially of missionaries, who speak of Hindus bowing down to wood and stone. Such critics, they say, ought to understand that it is not the material image which the so-called "heathen" worship, but the divine being whom the image symbolizes. Unfortunately we have a striking testimony, in support of the missionary assertion, not

---

[1] Οὕτω διέγνω τὸ ἄρρητον ἄγαλμα τοῦ Αἰῶνος ὑπὸ τοῦ θεοῦ κατεχόμενον, ὃν Ἀλεξανδρεῖς ἐτίμησαν, Ὄσιριν ὄντα καὶ Ἀδῶνιν ὁμοῦ, κατὰ μυστικήν, ὡς ἀληθῶς φάναι, θεοκρασίαν. There is some question what θεοκρασία means. It is commonly used by modern scholars to mean that fusion of different deities which was characteristic of the last phase of ancient paganism. Such a meaning would fit this passage—Aion and Osiris and Adonis are all mystically understood by the Alexandrines to be one being. But Reitzenstein (*Das iranische Erlösungsmysterium*, p. 98) has maintained that always elsewhere in ancient religious literature θεοκρασία means something quite different, a mystical union of the human person with the deity. And if in this passage κατὰ μυστικὴν θεοκρασίαν is taken with διέγνω, not with Ἀλεξανδρεῖς ἐτίμησαν or ὄντα, that meaning is possible here. My translation follows this supposition. If Reitzenstein is right, the current use of θεοκρασία by modern scholars is wrong.

35

Holy Images

from a missionary, not from a Christian, not from a European, but from a Hindu of such militant nationalism as the late Lala Lajpat Rai. That eminent Indian leader adhered to the sect of the Arya Somaj, founded by the holy man, Swami Dayananda Saraswati, in the early part of the last century. The sect is, of course, numerous and powerful to-day in Northern India, and makes it a principal part of its programme to combat idolatry, which it declares to be a perversion of the original Hinduism of the Vedas. In his book on the Arya Somaj Lala Lajpat Rai describes how the founder, Dayananda, first got his insight into the wrongness of idolatry. He was set, as a lad of fourteen, to watch an image of the god Shiva, in a temple at night. He saw a mouse run over the god's body and the god remain motionless. The shock convinced him, Lajpat Rai wrote, that "the image could not be Shiva himself, as was taught by the priesthood."[1] Note that the belief is here stated to have been, not merely a popular belief held by the simple and uninstructed, but a belief which the authoritative exponents of the religion, the priests, taught as true.

Rudolf Otto has given in his book on the Aryan deities a description of how the Indian mind, as he understands it, envisages the relation of the god to the material objects in which he is believed to reside:

"The immanent *numen* (he writes) is connected by a mystical community of being with his material vehicle, which we might describe in terms of Dogmatic Theology as a *communicatio idiomatum* or an *unio sacramentalis*. The deity of the *vishnu* class who sits in a *sālagrāma* stone, is somehow one with it; similarly the *vishnu* deity who sits in a *tulasi* plant or a *nyagrodha* tree. Each material

[1] *The Arya Samaj* (Longmans, Green & Co., 1915), p. 8.

Hindu Theory of Indwelling

thing is, the later dogmatics of Vishnu religion teach, his *āvesa*. That is something more, something other, than a mere *rupa* (form in which a deity appears) or a mere habitation. The things carry him as 'power' in themselves. They do not simply represent the *numen*: in a certain way they are the *numen*."[1]

"What we are accustomed to call *fetishism*," he says a few pages further on, "the coincidence of the *numen* with the object worshipped, is a permanent characteristic of Vishnu religion. True, the characteristic appears in some degree wherever a *numen* is reverenced in an image. But the Vaishnavas (worshippers of Vishnu) have framed a special sacramental theory about it, in their dogma of the *arcā*. The *arcā*, the object worshipped, may be in the first instance one 'self-constituted.' Obviously there come under this heading old nature-fetishes, such as ammonite fossils large and small, which are worshipped as Vishnu and called *sālagrāma* stones: or they may be particular trees, or plants such as the *tulasi*. . . . Then come the artificially-shaped images in the temples. These *arcās* are defined as 'embodiments' of Vishnu. He is one with them to the extent that in his condescension he really shares in their low mode of being. Lokācharyā says of them: 'Although omniscient, Vishnu shows himself in his *arcās* as without knowledge; although spirit, he shows himself as material; although very Lord, he shows himself as in the power of men; although almighty he shows himself as weak; although without needs, he shows himself as one who needs tendance; although invisible to sense, he shows himself as one who can be touched.' "[2]

A Greek lad, one thinks, would hardly have had a similar shock to that experienced by Swami Dayananda,

[1] *Gottheit und Gottheiten der Arier*, p. 84. [2] Ibid., pp. 90, 91.

37

Holy Images

if he had seen a mouse run over an image of Apollo. He would not to that extent have ever imagined an identity between the image and the god. But even as against the Greek view the mockery of the Jewish books cannot be considered wide of the mark, in so far as the Greeks believed that by doing something to an image you could please a god, or make a god hear. Only one has to recognize that the argument: "It is absurd to worship an image because an image is wood or stone made by the hands of man," if taken as an argument addressed to the pagan image-worshipper is a begging of the question. The point at issue is whether the rites believed to have caused the god to enter and animate the image do effect that, or whether the idea that by doing something to the image of a person you can act upon that person at a distance is true. Of course, if you take the rationalist view, or the Hebrew prophetic view, that the rites effect nothing at all and that the idea of real beings who could be pleased by what is done to an image, is a delusion, then, when you watch the worshipper bow down to what you hold to be mere wood and stone, you see him do something supremely ridiculous. The mockery expresses truly the aspect which, *on your supposition*, the action wears. But the worshipper does not accept your supposition: he believes that the image is no longer mere wood and stone, that there is a god inside it, or that a virtue proceeding from the god is in it, so that the god can, through it, perform acts of power, or that there is, at any rate, some magical connexion between the image and the god. The argument that the image is necessarily futile because it is of material substance and made by hands of men is quite inconclusive. The worshipper knows that well enough. But for him the past history of the material composing the image no more

Second Objection to Idolatry

proves that it is not now the vehicle of a consciousness than the past history of your body proves that it is not now animate. At a certain moment the salts and other substances composing your body became the vehicle of a personality, and at a certain moment the wood and stone shaped by the hands of men became, the worshipper believes, the abode or instrument of a god. It all depends on the question whether the rites supposed to have charged the image with the presence or power of a god really had effect. And we shall see that, while the mockery of idolatry in the Old Testament passages quoted is based on the conviction that they did not have effect, there is another line of attack on idolatry, largely followed by the early Christians, which admits that they may have had effect. But before we come to that we must consider a ground of objection raised to idolatry in the Old Testament quite different from the charge that it falsely supposes a block of inanimate material to be animated—the condemnation of it because it makes a similitude of God.

Attention was called earlier in our discussion to the two different lines along which idolatry was attacked in the Old Testament, according as the idolatry in question was the worship of false gods or the worship of Jehovah. All the mockery of which specimens were given from Isaiah and the Epistle of Jeremy and the Book of Wisdom referred to the worship of the pagan gods by pagans. It was in regard to the worship of Jehovah by means of an image in Israel itself that the wickedness of making a similitude was declared. Pious Israelites would not presumably have minded that a low anthropomorphic or theriomorphic conception should be entertained of Osiris or Marduk or Dagon, but that Jehovah should be repre-

Holy Images

sented in visible form as a man or as a beast—that was the abominable thing.

"Take heed unto yourselves," Moses says to the children of Israel in the Book of Deuteronomy (iv. 15-18), "for ye saw no similitude on the day that Jehovah spoke unto you in Horeb out of the midst of the fire: lest ye corrupt yourselves and make you a graven image, the similitude of any figure, the likeness of male or female, the likeness of any beast that is on the earth, the likeness of any winged fowl that flieth in the air, the likeness of any fish that is in the waters beneath the earth." That this objection to idolatry was quite distinct from the other objection—the objection based on the false attribution of life to an inanimate material thing—may be obscured for some people by the fact that in many cases of idolatry the practice might be attacked on both grounds. If the image of a calf was set up to represent Jehovah (as in the Northern Israelite kingdom), that might be denounced both because Jehovah was in no wise like a calf:

"They turned their glory into the similitude of a calf that eateth hay." (Psalm cvi. 20.)

and also because men treated the image of the calf as if it were alive:

"They sin more and more, and have made them molten images of their silver, even idols according to their own devising, all of them work of the craftsman: men that sacrifice kiss calves." (Hosea xiii. 2.)

Or again, while the worship of idols by pagans might be ridiculed, because it proceeded on the supposition that the idols were alive, it might also be condemned because the worship directed to things in the shape of a man or an

Sanctity Without Similitude

animal ought to have been directed to the God of whom no such similitude could be rightly conceived. In such cases the two grounds of objection went together, but there were other cases to which one ground applied and the other did not. Where the object of worship was aniconic, an unshaped stone or a board, there was no attempted similitude, but there was the attribution of a quality like life and consciousness to an inanimate thing: contrariwise, if an image were made which purported to show the similitude of Jehovah, even if it were not worshipped, even if it were treated as an inanimate piece of matter, it would come under condemnation, on the second ground. The fields covered by the two objections overlapped, but they did not coincide.

And here one must notice something which may appear very odd. The prophetic Hebrew religion did not shrink from the idea of a supernatural virtue inhering in a material object, when there was no similitude. The worship of images in likeness of man, the images of Zeus and Athena and Apollo, might seem to us to mark an advance to a higher stage of human culture beyond the savage's tendance of some fetish, a bundle of rags or a stone without any animal form. But from the standpoint of Hebrew religion it is not an advance; it is a step deeper into impiety. The savage's belief that supernatural virtue resides in some aniconic object is not so far removed from the truth as the Greeks' worship of an idol. Hebrew religion did, of course, regard as wicked the worship of the Ashērīm—the word which is translated "groves" in our Authorized Version, but which apparently means poles or pillars set up to represent a goddess—because here the worship was addressed to another deity than Jehovah. But where the power in question was that of

Holy Images

Jehovah, while it was wicked to connect it with any material object which showed the similitude of man or animal, no objection was felt to connecting it with an aniconic object. The ark, for instance, was credited with being charged with a dangerous supernatural virtue similar to that which the pagans attributed to certain images: Uzzah was struck dead when he touched it, although he did so with an innocent intention.[1] The supernatural healing power which Elisha could call into action, might reside in his staff: Gehazi carries the prophet's staff to lay it upon the dead boy in order to restore him to life, though in this case the staff failed to convey the power.[2] The power did, however, continue to reside in the dead bones of Elisha, so that contact with them restored a corpse to life.[3] The same principle would be seen in the idea of holy ground—a particular bit of material earth which was charged with numinous quality, and so might be touched only with certain precautions. To touch Sinai at the time Jehovah rested upon it was forbidden on pain of death.[4] A heathen, ridiculed by a Jew because he believed that divine power resided in an image made by the hands of men, might have retorted that it was just as reasonable to believe that power resided in a wooden image as to believe that it resided in

[1] 2 Samuel vi. 6, 7. It may be urged that the Hebrew writer does not represent Uzzah as having been struck dead by any virtue residing in the ark, but by Jehovah, Uzzah's touching the ark being only the occasion which provoked Jehovah's anger. That is true, and important to note as indicating the character of Jewish religion. Yet it is because some quality of holiness attaches to the ark that to touch it provokes Jehovah's anger, and so the heathen might have argued, in regard to their idols, that the power proceeding from them was not that of the material wood or stone, but that of the deity, which the deity put forth on the occasion of something being done to the image.

[2] 2 Kings iv. 29–31. [3] 2 Kings xiii. 21. [4] Exodus xix. 12, 13.

Images in Old Israel

a wooden box, equally made by the hands of men. To the Jew it made all the difference that in the case of the ark there was no similitude. And it is curious to observe that in Islam we find an analogous difference in regard to iconic and aniconic objects of religious regard. The tendance of the old black stone at Mecca—to stroke it is part of the pilgrim's devotions—has sometimes been pointed to as inconsistent with the Moslem horror of idolatry. But the old black stone is aniconic; there is no similitude. Islam has also its holy places, its holy carpets, and so on.[1]

It is not necessary for me to go into the inquiry, which indeed would demand special knowledge to which I have no claim, how far back in the history of Israel the condemnation of idolatry goes. It is admitted, even according to the most rigidly traditional belief regarding the Biblical record, that a large proportion of the Israelite people before the latter days of the kingdom of Judah, believed that the worship of images was acceptable to Jehovah. In the Northern Kingdom the worship of the calf at Bethel was the state worship of the national God. In the Kingdom of Judah before the time of Hezekiah there were many people who offered homage to the brazen serpent said to have been made by the command of Moses.[2] David in the story has teraphim in his house, a sacred image in human form.[3] The fact of this image-

---

[1] What has just been said may be remembered in connexion with the Catholic adoration of the consecrated Host. Whether the Catholic belief is true or not this is not the place to discuss, but when Protestants attack the Catholic practice as "idolatry," it should be taken into account that the object of worship is aniconic. No Catholic supposes that Christ is *like* a wafer, that anything in the Host which the senses of sight and touch apprehend is an attribute of Christ.

[2] 2 Kings xviii. 4.   [3] 1 Samuel xix. 13.

Holy Images

worship in ancient Israel is not denied by the traditional doctrine. It is only asserted that the Second Commandment had already been promulgated long before by Moses, and that image-worship was an apostasy from the Law of Jehovah given to the fathers. The dominant critical view is, of course, that no more than a small nucleus of the legislation in the Pentateuch can go back to Moses; to attribute even the Ten Commandments to him would now be generally considered uncritical. Some critics apparently believe that the idea which condemned a *graven* image arose before a *molten* image was also considered wrong, because a graven image was itself shaped by men's hands, whereas in the case of a molten image, although the mould had been made by man, the metal had taken shape of itself in the mould. Perhaps we shall never be able to say with any certainty how much of the Law was earlier than the eighth-century prophets, how far, when Hosea denounced idolatry at Bethel, he was an innovator, and how far the restorer of a religion which had become corrupted. One may only note that a Roman Catholic scholar of such unquestioned competence as Lagrange can still argue that the success of the prophets, in securing the survival of Judaism, is intelligible only if their message met a knowledge in the heart of the people, that the prophets had behind them a recognized, but violated, law.[1] For our purposes it is enough to take note of the fact that when Judaism was there as the special religion which survived the Exile, whether that Judaism came into being earlier than the eighth-century prophets or not before the end of the Kingdom of Judah, the attitude of the religion to image-worship was expressed in the second of the Ten Com-

[1] M. J. Lagrange, O.P., *Le Judaïsme avant Jésus-Christ*, pp. 4–8.

Jewish Prohibition of Idolatry

mandments. This Commandment indeed says nothing about the folly of treating an inanimate thing as alive. It speaks only of making a similitude—"the likeness of any form that is in heaven above, or that is in the earth beneath, or that is in the water under the earth." That is intelligible when one remembers that the objection to idolatry on the ground that it treated wood and stone as alive, had reference mainly to the worship of false gods by pagans: the wrongness of a similitude was the objection urged against idolatry in Israel, and it was to Israel that the Commandment was addressed. But what was it precisely that the Commandment prohibited? Was it only the worshipping of an image? Or was it forbidden to make the representation of certain things whether for purposes of worship or not? With regard to this question, different views have prevailed. We must proceed to the consideration of these in our next lecture.

LECTURE II

In our last lecture we were looking at the two grounds on which idolatry was denounced in the Old Testament, that it treated an inanimate piece of matter as if it were alive, that it made a similitude of a living thing to represent God. By the time that the Ten Commandments had come to be regarded as the Law of Jehovah, given through Moses, whether that was not till the latter days of the Kingdom of Judah or very much earlier, the Second Commandment, according to our mode of distribution,[1] was there, a plain prohibition of image-worship on the latter of the two grounds. But while image-worship is plainly forbidden by that Commandment, in some respects the Commandment is ambiguous. The words: "Thou shalt not make unto thee a graven image, nor the likeness of any form that is in heaven above, or that is in the earth beneath, or that is in the water under the earth," might be taken to prohibit, not only the worshipping of an image, but the making of one at all, the representation, by sculpture or painting, of any visible object. As ordinarily taken by Christians, the prohibition in these words is meant to be understood as qualified by the succeeding words: "Thou shalt not bow down thyself unto them nor serve them," so that the meaning would not be: "It is wrong in any circumstances to make an image of any visible object," but: "It is wrong to

[1] The Roman Church reckons what we call the Second Commandment as part of the First, and divides our Tenth Commandment into two, to make up the number ten.

The Second Commandment

make an image with a view to worshipping it." It can hardly be denied, I suppose, that the Hebrew may well bear this meaning. In Hebrew, phrases are often put in mere sequence, of which one, in a classical or modern language, would be given grammatically a relation of logical dependence upon the other. Where we say: "Thou shalt not make an image in order to worship it," a Hebrew could say: "Thou shalt not make an image; thou shalt not worship it." While, however, the Commandment in Hebrew may quite well bear this meaning, it need not necessarily do so: it might be taken as prohibiting the making of images, even when there was no intention of worshipping them. But no one, so far as I know, has ever taken the Commandment to prohibit the making of an image of any visible object at all in the sky or on the earth or in the water, although that is what the words, taken literally, do prohibit. Even where it has been regarded as wrong not only to worship images, but to make them, the prohibition has been qualified in one or other of two ways. One: the prohibition has been understood to apply to the images of men and animals only, not of vegetable or mineral objects; or, secondly, to apply only to the representation of such objects, whether animal or not, as men might be tempted to worship, such as the sun or moon. The words of the Second Commandment say, of course, nothing about living creatures in distinction from other objects of sky and land and sea, nor do they qualify in any way, unless it is by the following clause which prohibits the worship of an image, the general prohibition to make an image of anything at all. But men have evidently found it unthinkable that God forbade them to make a pictorial representation of anything at all, literally anything. Their reading of one

Holy Images

or other qualification into the Commandment was an act of their own sense of what was necessitated by reason. The Jews, in the times immediately before, and immediately after, the Christian era, apparently understood the prohibition of the Law to apply to images of all living creatures, but of living creatures only. This is implied in the statements of Josephus: when he describes the embroideries in the Tabernacle, he notes that the thing which in their rich designs had to be avoided was any animal form.[1] He himself, Josephus tells us, when, as a young man, he held a command in Galilee, urged the Council of the city of Tiberias to destroy the palace built by Herod Antipas, because it had in it representations of living creatures[2]—which was contrary to the Law. It caused grave trouble in Jerusalem when Pontius Pilate brought Roman troops into the city, because their standards had on them busts of the Emperor.[3] Another and earlier occasion of trouble had been the action of Herod the Great in placing a golden eagle above the chief gate of his new Temple.[4] It is against the Law, Josephus explains, for there to be in the Temple any image or bust or any work of art bearing the name of a living creature.[5]

These statements of Josephus are borne out by the coinage of the Jewish kings, both the Hasmoneans and the house of Herod. They show representations of a number of natural objects—an olive wreath, a flower, a palm, a bunch of grapes, a star—and a number of manufactured objects—an anchor, a cup, a helmet, a lyre—but of no men or animals, except only that Herod,

---

[1] Arch., iii. § 113, 126. [2] ζῴων μορφάς, Life, § 65.
[3] Arch., xviii. 55. [4] Arch., xvii. § 151.
[5] ζῴου τινος ἐπώνυμον ἔργον, Bellum, i. § 650.

Rabbinic Rules

who tried to decorate the Temple with an eagle, put an eagle on some of his small bronze coins.

So far all appears plain. The rule: "No representation of a living creature" is a simple and intelligible one, whether rightly deducible from the written Law or not. But now come the difficulties. The rule seems quite abandoned when we come to the Rabbinic tradition which began to be put in writing about one hundred years after the death of Josephus, and to be replaced by a set of quite different, and much more complicated, rules.

One: No representation of any object at all is to be made as a representation of God. The distinction between living creatures and inanimate objects does not here come in: representations of sun or moon or stars, of seas or hills or rivers, are equally prohibited, if they purport to be images of God.

Two: There are certain other beings beside God of which no representation may be made. The Hebrew of Exodus xx. 23, is, literally translated, "Ye shall not make *with me* gods of silver or gods of gold." "*With* me." The curious scrutiny of the Rabbis caught in this phrase. What does "*with me*" mean? Rabbi Ishmael (early second century) determined that the text meant: "Ye shall not represent those who are with me as gods of silver or gods of gold." Those who are with God are His servants, who minister before Him in heaven, and so the text forbids making a representation of angels or of Ophannim (the living Wheels of the Divine Chariot) or of Cherubim. Other later Rabbis, however, maintained that the phrase "with me" indicated the material heavenly bodies; but there was a difference of opinion whether the prohibition applied to all the heavenly bodies, or only to some. One Rabbi (Rab Shesheth, about A.D. 260) pronounced that

Holy Images

representations of other heavenly bodies were permitted, but not of the sun and moon. It seems to have been generally agreed at this time that representations of the sun and moon were forbidden. No doubt this view was largely due to the fact that sun and moon were especially objects of pagan worship: the phrase "with me" was therefore stretched in order to apply to them. It was a difficulty that the great first-century Rabbi, Gamaliel II, so the Rabbinic tradition affirmed, had had pictures of the moon in its various phases painted on the walls of his upper chamber. This was got over by explaining that he had them for the purpose of giving directions for those observations of the new moon by which some religious festivals were fixed: this, it was argued, was sufficient justification.

The most common Rabbinic opinion was that an image might be made of any living creature, except a human being, and this seems to have been the view of the great medieval Jewish philosopher, Maimonides. There are a number of allusions to embroidery in which the figures of animals appear, as of something quite inoffensive—lions are particularly mentioned. The only creatures beside man sometimes mentioned as creatures which it is impious to portray are dragons. Even in the case of dragons it was not clear that all dragons were forbidden: one Rabbi (latter part of fifth century) gave it as his judgment that the prohibition applied only to a dragon which had fins upon its neck: if its neck was quite smooth, without fins, an image of it he pronounced to be permissible.[1] Why dragons should have been singled out in this way is to-day a matter of conjecture. Someone

---

[1] References to the Rabbinical passages cited will be found in Strack and Billerbeck: *Kommentar zum Neuen Testament*, vol. iv. pp. 389-94.

Permitted and Forbidden Images

has suggested that it was because the Emperor Trajan had dragon emblems upon his standards. Mr. Elmslie, in his edition of *Abodah Zarah*,[1] the tract in the *Mishnah* on the problems of conduct presented to Jews by environing paganism, thinks it more likely that it was because there was the worship of a sea-monster (the *ketos*, from which Perseus rescued Andromeda) established at Joppa. We can only penetrate by guessing into the tortuous intricacies of the Rabbinic mind. In any case, the tract just referred to shows that the sun, the moon, and dragons formed a group of things ordinarily thought of as those whose portrayal was wicked. If a man finds utensils, says a passage in the *Abodah Zarah*, upon which any of these things is depicted, the utensils must be cast into the Dead Sea. The figures of men are not mentioned: it was probably taken for granted that those were unlawful.

Was there any feeling amongst the Rabbis that an image in the round was more heinous than a picture in the flat? Such a distinction has, of course, been made by the Greek Orthodox Church since medieval times. But in the Greek Church the distinction does not seem yet to have been made at the time of the Iconoclastic controversy in the eighth and ninth centuries. There is a trace of it in a Christian writer of the fourth century, St. Epiphanius. The Christian Father is dealing with the origins of idolatry. Its beginning he puts down to Serug, one of the line going from Shem to Abraham in Genesis xi. "With Serug, idolatry and paganism ('Ἑλληνισμός), he says, "took their start amongst men. It was, however,

[1] *The Mishna on Idolatry, Abodah Zarah*, edited with translation, vocabulary, and notes, by W. A. L. Elmslie (Cambridge University Press, 1911).

Holy Images

so far, not a matter of images and the graving of stones or of wood, or of figures fashioned in silver or any other substance: it was only in the way of colour-painting and pictures that the mind of man devised for itself evil." But with Serug's grandson Terah, the step deeper into evil is made. "From that time," Epiphanius says, "there began the fashioning of statues from moulded mud by the craft of the worker in clay, according to the art of this same Terah."[1]

It seems possible that the Christian is here taking over a piece of current Jewish *midrash*.[2] Yet it may have been a *midrash* invented by some Christian, and, if taken from the Jews, one would conjecture it came from a Hellenistic rather than a Rabbinical Jew. For it seems based upon the Greek legend regarding the origin of the art of modelling images in clay. According to this, the art began with Butades of Sicyon who discovered a profile sketch made by his daughter of her lover; she had marked the edge of his shadow on a wall, obtaining thus what the Greeks called a *skiographia*. The idea occurred to Butades of filling up the space inside the outline with clay so that the figure stood out in bas-relief.[3] Portraiture in the flat had given place to portraiture in the round. That the *midrash* given by Epiphanius was suggested by this Greek legend is indicated by the fact that in a parallel passage in another work of Epiphanius (*Ankyrotos*, 102) he actually uses the word *skiographia* in connexion with the origins of idolatry. "When this innovation," that passage

[1] I. 6 (Dindorf, I. p. 286.)
[2] A *midrash* is a Rabbinical commentary on scripture, which in many cases expands the narrative with old legendary or new imaginative matter.
[3] Pliny, *Nat. Hist.*, xxxv. § 151. The same story with variations and other names is told by Athenagoras, *Libellus pro Christ*, 17.

Butades and Shadow-sketches

says, "was made by men through the evil work of daemons, the idols were first drawn in *shadow-sketches* (ἐν σκιογραφίαις). Next, everybody passed on to his children, for their homage, the products of the particular art which he himself exercised, and by which he got his living. In the material with which his particular craft dealt each man fashioned gods; the potter in clay, the carpenter in wood, the goldsmith in gold, and so forth."

In Rabbinical literature there seems something like the distinction made between a picture in the flat and an image in the round in the prescription in the Talmud that you may use, for sealing, a signet ring with the raised image of a man upon it, because when you seal with it, the figure in the wax will be concave and therefore not be so much an image as a hollow. The signet with the raised figure on it may not, however, be worn. On the other hand it is permissible to wear a signet with the figure sunk upon it, but you must not use such a signet for sealing.[1]

But it is more expressly intimated that a distinction was felt between a picture and a sculptured figure in a saying of Rabbi Abbaye (who lived in Babylonia, A.D. 273–339). He is answering an objector who adduces the case of an earlier Rabbi who possessed the repre-

[1] *Abodah Zarah* (Talmud), 5, 2.

It has sometimes been asserted that Jews in the Middle Ages never had seals. Professor Loewe points out to me that this is demonstrably untrue. One interesting example to the contrary is a deed conveying a piece of ground to Merton College, Oxford, which bears the seal of the vendor, Jacob son of Moses. The device of the seal includes a lion. Professor Loewe refers also to a French-Jewish writer of the thirteenth century, who says: "It is now a custom among the Jews of England to have seals *with a human face (parsôf = πρόσωπον),*" and a Jewish seal has actually been discovered (at Edinburgh) which bears a human head.

Holy Images

sentation of a heavenly being made for him by a pagan, and who was adjured by Rabbi Samuel to deface it. Rabbi Abbaye justifies the objection taken by Rabbi Samuel by saying that the representation was a projecting figure, not a flat picture, rather implying that, had it been a picture, there would not have been much harm in it.[1]

In the Book of Ezekiel a description is given, in two passages, of the Cherubs or "Living Creatures (*Hayyôth*)" who accompany the throne of Jehovah. In the first passage (i. 5-13) we are told that there are four of them, and that each of the four has four faces, looking in four different directions—the face of a man, the face of a lion, the face of an ox, and the face of an eagle.[2] In the second passage (x. 14) the four faces are given (in the Massoretic text, which is probably here corrupt) as that of a cherub, that of a man, that of a lion, and that of an eagle. A cherub takes the place of the ox. In regard to these four living creatures we have a curious Rabbinic pronouncement[3] that, while it is illegitimate to represent all the four *hayyôth* together, one or other of them may be represented by himself. This, however, seems only to mean that you may make the picture or image of a lion or an eagle by itself, because in that case it will be taken to represent an ordinary earthly lion or eagle, whereas, if they were combined in a group with a man and an ox, or all combined together in a single head, it would become the representation of a heavenly being, which is forbidden. We must not suppose that it would

---
[1] *Rōsh hash-Shānāh*, 24b.

[2] It is to be noted that in the Book of Revelation the corresponding four Living Creatures have each only a single face, one the face of a man, another the face of a lion, another the face of an ox, and another the face of an eagle (iv. 7).

[3] *Responsa* of Rabbi Abbaye in *Rōsh hash-Shānāh*, 24b.

The Living Creatures of Ezekiel

be legitimate to represent the Living Creature with the face of a man by himself, because that would be ruled out by the general prohibition of making any images of the human form. Some scruple seems to have been felt about the ox,[1] because, as we have just seen, in the second description given by Ezekiel, the face given in the first description as that of an ox, is given as that of a cherub, and it might therefore be deduced that the figure of an ox was equivalent to that of a heavenly being.

The facts we have hitherto surveyed have long been known, and thirty years ago the conclusion which it seemed safe to draw from them was that a severer view prevailed in the Judaism of the earlier centuries of the Christian era than in medieval Judaism. The great authority on the earlier Judaism, Emil Schürer, could say in 1907: "Judaism rejected all representations of men or animals."[2] Yet some archaeological evidence known even as far as the middle of the last century should have shown that the prohibition against depicting animals was by no means universally observed by the Jews of the earlier Christian centuries, and recent excavation has brought surprises. Jewish catacombs in Rome have some of their chambers decorated with paintings which include representations of animals. In the catacomb of the Vigna Randanini (already explored in the 60's of the nineteenth century), we find, engraved on marble doors, chickens, rams and bulls. One bull is on the sepulchral tablet of a doctor of the law. There is also a chamber adorned with paintings in which birds appear. The same catacomb has yielded fragments of a sarcophagus in

[1] *Hagigah* 13b; *Sukkah* 5b.
[2] *Geschichte das Jüdischen Volkes im Zeitalter Jesu Christi* (fourth edition, 1907), ii. p. 65.

Holy Images

which winged gryphons are combined with specifically Jewish emblems.[1] A few years ago another Jewish catacomb was discovered beneath the Villa Torlonia, still richer in paintings, belonging, it is believed (though apparently without any certain ground), to the early part of the second century. In these, side by side with Jewish emblems (the roll of the law, the seven-branched candlestick, etc.), are dolphins, lions' heads, peacocks, a ram, the sun and the moon.[2] It might be suggested that if Jews in Rome had such paintings to decorate their sepulchres, they probably did not execute them themselves, but only allowed pagan artists to work in their traditional manner. We have, however, the sarcophagus of a Jew whose profession was that of ζoögraphos, "painter of living things." [3]

---

[1] J. B. Frey, *Corpus Inscriptionum Judaicarum*; Garrucci, *Civiltà Cattolica*, Ser. v, vol. vi (1863), p. 104; *Cimitero degli antichi Ebrei in Vigna Randanini*, 1862, p. 9.

[2] Beyer and Lietzmann, *Die judische Katakombe der Villa Torlonia*, 1930; J. B. Frey, *Rivista di Archeologia Christiana* viii (1931), pp. 301–314, pp. 360 ff. On the doubtfulness of the dating, see W. Elliger, *Zur Entstehung d. christ. Bildkunst*, pp. 22 ff.

In two cubicles connected with the catacomb of the Vigna Randanini are paintings in which not only animals, but beings in human form are depicted—a winged Victory offering a garland to a naked youth, a figure of Fortune holding a cornucopia, the *genii* of the Four Seasons. These have commonly been adduced as Jewish, but Father J. B. Frey has indicated ground for believing that the cubicles in question are pagan, originally unconnected with the Jewish catacomb.

[3] Found near the Vigna Randanini. 'Ενθάδε κιτε (κεῖται) Εὐδόξιος ζωογράφος· ἐν εἰρήνη ἡ κύ[μησις] (κοίμησις) [αὐτοῦ], "Here lies Eudoxios, painter: may his sleep be in peace."

W. Elliger (*Zur Entstehung und frühen Entwickelung der christlichen Kunst*, Leipzig, 1934, p. 15) conjectures that the representations of the human form in Jewish catacombs and on Jewish sarcophagi were made for proselytes who had been pagans, but the conjecture seems to me unnecessary.

Jewish Decorative Painting

At Gamast in Tunisia, near the site of ancient Carthage, Jewish sepulchral chambers have been discovered, decorated with painted stucco figures in relief. These represent winged *genii*, horsemen, and a vintage scene with men carrying amphoras and a female figure.[1]

The cases so far referred to might be explained as works executed for individual Jews who happened to be indifferent in matters of religion: such an explanation would not fit the more surprising cases in which representations of animals, and even of men, are used to decorate synagogues. In 1905 and 1907 the ruins of a number of synagogues in Galilee, belonging to the second or third century of our era, were excavated by H. Kohl and C. Watzinger. One of these was the synagogue of Capernaum, not probably the actual building in which Jesus spoke, but one built about A.D. 200 upon the same site. In the decorations of these synagogues there were found, not only lions, eagles, and dolphins, but winged *genii*, cupids carrying garlands, a vintage scene with human figures and other representations of the human form.[2]

In the synagogue of Hammam-Lif near the site of Carthage (discovered in 1883) the decoration includes beasts, birds, and fishes.

But the most notable case of paintings in a synagogue so far discovered is that of the synagogue at Dura (Europos) on the Euphrates, excavated in 1932 and 1933

---

[1] P. Delattre, *Gamast ou la nécropole juive de Carthage* (1895); H. Leclercq, article "Gamast" in the *Dict. d'Archéol. Chrétienne*, vol. vi.

[2] References to the literature of the subject will be found in the article by Father J. B. Frey, entitled *La Question des Images chez les Juifs* in *Biblica*, xv (1934), pp. 265 ff., to which I am under special obligation in this account of Jewish art in the first centuries of our era. See also Cabrol et Leclercq, *Diction. d'Archéol. Chrétienne*, art. "Judaïsme" by H. Leclercq.

Holy Images

by the Americans and French (see plate i). Here there is no shrinking from portrayal of the human form. The synagogue is precisely dated by an inscription as having been built in the year A.D. 245. It is decorated with a series of frescoes representing Old Testament prophets and scenes from Old Testament story. These include Abraham preparing to sacrifice Isaac, Jehovah Himself being represented by a Hand emerging from the clouds, Jacob's dream, Moses and the burning bush, the passage of the Red Sea, the capture of the Ark by the Philistines and its return in the cart drawn by two cows, Elijah and the widow of Zarephath, the miracle of Mount Carmel, and the vision of Ezekiel.

"Moses," says Professor Rostovtzeff, "is presented here somewhat in the character of one of the great founders of new religions of the ancient world, as a canonized and almost deified hero, founder of the Jewish religion—a counterpart in some degree to Buddha and Christ. The idea is uncanonical. The semi-divinization of Moses is stressed by the square nimbus which surrounds his head, light in the pictures which show him living, black in that which shows him after his death."[1]

The artists (there were at least three) who painted these frescoes appear to have been Jews, one accompanies his pictures with words in Aramaic, and another writes, in Greek characters, near his pictures of the Ark, the Hebrew word for "ark," *arôn*. The art of these works is on a higher level than that of the early Christian catacombs, and C. H. Kraeling indicates the possibility that we may ultimately discover early Christian painting

[1] M. Rostovtzeff, *Dura-Europus and its Art*, Clarendon Press (1938), p. 108.

[*By courtesy of the Gallery of Fine Arts, Yale University*

PLATE I.—FIGURE FROM THE DURA FRESCOES (ABRAHAM ?)

The Frescoes at Dura-Europus

to have continued the tradition of preceding Jewish artists.[1]

While, however, all these products of Jewish art in the early centuries of our era prove conclusively that the contemporary Rabbis did not by any means all disapprove of the representation of animals and men, so long as the figures were not made in order to be worshipped, the more rigorous view, that they were wrong, must also have continued to be upheld by some authorities in the community. Some paintings of animals in the synagogues of Palestine seem to have been deliberately defaced before the synagogues fell into ruin, and Watzinger conjectures that this was done by Jews when the stricter view came to prevail.[2] At Dura the older synagogue which preceded that of 245 seems to have been free from any representation of men or animals.

But it was not only a problem for the Jews in the ancient world, what images they might, and what they might not, make: it was also a problem to what extent, in what way, they should show their abhorrence of the images made by others—the images which were there all round them in every Greek town in the streets, the gymnasia, the baths, the private houses. Here, again, there were evidently varieties of opinion, severer views, and views relatively easy-going. A story, for instance,

---

[1] *Excavations at Dura-Europos, Sixth Season,* 1932-3, Yale University Press, p. 383. What Kraeling suggests as a possible future hypothesis, that Christian art originated from an earlier Jewish art, has actually been maintained already by O. Wulff, *Altchrist. u. byzant. Kunst,* i. pp. 45 ff.

[2] Cohl and Watzinger, *Antike Synagogen in Galiläa.* (Wissensch. Veröffent. d. deutsch. Orientgesellschaft. Heft 29), pp. 202, 203. E. L. Sukenik, *Ancient Synagogues in Palestine and Greece.* (Oxford University Press, 1934), pp. 63-5.

Holy Images

is told of Rabbi Gamaliel II (about A.D. 90) that when asked by a heathen philosopher how he could reconcile with the Jewish Law his bathing in a bath-house called after Aphrodite and decorated with an image of the goddess, he answered: "I did not go on to her domain: she came on to mine: no one would say: 'The bath-house was made for Aphrodite'; Aphrodite was made as an ornament for the bath-house."[1] Although the query is put into the mouth of a heathen, the story no doubt indicates that the question, whether a pious Jew could consistently resort to heathen baths, with their array of images and statues, was one which exercised Rabbinic casuistry. Another story about the same Rabbi Gamaliel shows, so Strack and Billerbeck think, that his practice of resorting to heathen bath-houses did cause some scandal in the contemporary Jewish community. The story is that when he once went with a proselyte companion to Ascalon, the proselyte took his bath in the sea, but Rabbi Gamaliel went to the public bath-house. Afterwards, to cover this action of his, his son-in-law, another Rabbi, used to deny the fact and affirm, falsely, that he had been present on the occasion, and that Rabbi Gamaliel had had his dip only in the sea.[2]

There was one species of pagan imagery which no one in that world could help having continually presented to his eyes—the current money with the figure of the reigning emperor or one of his deified predecessors upon it. We hear of a Rabbi, Nahum ben Simai (round about A.D. 260), who achieved the feat of never, his whole life long—so it was reported—looking at a heathen coin. This, of course, was an excpteional case, and Rabbi

[1] *Abodah Zarah*, iii. 4.
[2] Talmud, *Miqwaoth*, 6, 2; Strack and Billerbeck, iii. p. 492.

Avoidance of Pagan Images

Nahum's feat won him the surname of "the All-holiest."[1]

A prohibition to look at an idol or a statue in passing was derived from the verse in Leviticus (xix. 4): *"Turn ye not unto idols."* When Rabbi Nahum died, the images past which his corpse was carried on its way to the grave were (according to the ordinary understanding of the Hebrew) covered with mats in respect for his memory, because in life he had always avoided looking at anything of the sort.[2]

Professor Loewe has suggested to me that the coinage throws light on one enigmatic utterance of the *Abodah Zarah* (Mishnah)—that the only images made by pagans which a Jew was bound to taboo, were those in which the human figure carried in its hand a staff, a bird, or a ball, to which the Talmud adds a sword, a crown, a ring, an idol, or a snake. The figures of pagan deities on the coins (taken probably in most cases from some well-known image in a particular temple) are often characterized by emblems which may be described by the terms used in the Rabbinic book. Zeus, for instance, is frequently represented with a long sceptre, or as holding on his outstretched hand an eagle or an image of Victory. The most surprising case of the toleration of an image by Jews is that of the synagogue at Nehardea on the Euphrates, in which there actually stood the statue (*andriantē* = Greek ἀνδριάς) of a Sassanian king. The case must have caused heart-burnings in the community because it became evidently a stock subject of Rabbinic

---

[1] Palestinian Talmud, *Abodah Zarah*, 3, 42c, 5.

[2] Palestinian Talmud, *Abodah Zarah*, 3, 42b, 58. Professor H. Loewe has pointed out to me that the characters of the word translated "mats" may also stand for the word meaning "files," and he thinks it probable that what this passage affirms is that when Rabbi Nahum died, the figures on some money were defaced by filing.

Holy Images

discussion. Rabbi Abbaye (A.D. 273–339) seems to have regarded the statue in question as innocuous because it was not worshipped. A later Rabbi argued that the statue was put there by the Persian authorities and that to have ejected it might have been an act of culpable disrespect to the King.

In the Middle Ages, and up to our own times, carved figures of lions in the round have been allowed in some synagogues. A notable case was that of the synagogue at Ascoli; the wooden shrine in which the rolls of the Law were kept rested upon two crouching lions, whose manes and open mouths, we are told, gave a vivid appearance of real life. The ark was transferred in the sixteenth century to the synagogue at Pesaro, and eminent Rabbis raised no objection to it. In the following century some Rabbis did make pronouncements against lions in synagogues, and we have a reasoned defence of them by the Italian Rabbi, Graziano (died 1685), against the judgment of condemnation. Graziano had a family interest in the lions of Pesaro, as the shrine had at one time been in the care of his great-grandfather, the great Rabbi, Azriel Trabot.[1] D. Kaufmann tells us that carved lions are found placed conspicuously on the tops of Arks in several synagogues, and he knows of one in which they were the work of a Jewish artist in the nineteenth century.[2]

---

[1] The argument of Graziano in defence of the lions is given in the original Hebrew by D. Kaufmann in his article: "Art in the Synagogue," *Jewish Quarterly Review*, vol. ix (1896–7), pp. 254 ff.

[2] One enigmatic statement may be noted: "Solomon Ibn Adret is of opinion that no prohibition extends to the making of a lion for the purpose of healing, whether by a Jew or a non-Jew. Even a representation in relief is permitted." It is to be found in the *Shiltē hag-Gibbōrīm* relating to the Digest of Isaac al Fāsī compiled by Isaiah

Lions in Synagogues

It is to be noted that those who objected to lions in the synagogues, or any decoration in which animals were represented, now based their objection, not on the Second Commandment, but upon the liability of such representations to distract the minds of worshippers. This reason is plainly an afterthought, in order to provide a justification for a feeling which had originally been created by the prohibition authoritative in earlier generations, and which remained instinctive in the Jewish community; when the condemnation could no longer be based on the original ground, some other ground had to be found for it. The new ground is really absurd. Ordinary psychology would tell us that a detail of decoration repeatedly before the eyes of worshippers would become unnoticeable with familiarity. Can we imagine any member of the Church of England finding his attention to the Lessons diverted because the lectern is in the form of a carved eagle?

As we saw in our last lecture, the Greek world which surrounded the Jews from the days of Alexander did worship images in a sense which gave justification to the Jewish mockery. Yet we have to note that in the Greek world itself there arose, quite independently of Jewish suggestion, a protest against the prevailing image-worship, a thin stream of protest running on through the centuries which can be traced from the sixth century B.C. up to the time when the Christian Church had spread

Boaz (Warsaw, 1882), *Abodah Zarah*, ch. iii. fol. 19a. I am indebted to Dr. J. Leveen, of the British Museum, for having kindly traced this reference for me.

I do not know whether anyone with extensive knowledge of medical practice in the Middle Ages could say what this means, or how carved lions were applied.

Holy Images

through the Roman Empire and taken up the protest with a new loudness and passion. When we find writers of the popular philosophy in the second century A.D.—Dio Chrysostom and Maximus of Tyre—discuss the question whether images of the gods are right and offer for them a regular philosophic defence, we could infer, even if we had no independent knowledge of the fact, that the rightness of images had been widely criticized. No one puts forward an elaborate defence of something which has not been attacked. It may well be that at a time as late as the second century A.D. many people in the Greek world had become uneasy in their minds about image-worship precisely because the Jewish and Christian denunciation of it was generally known. Yet we cannot say that Dio Chrysostom and Maximus of Tyre were thinking specially about Jews or Christians: both these writers felt themselves too much the representatives of the pure Hellenic tradition to be much troubled because some Hellenic institution was disliked by Orientals or people with an Oriental religion. It was probably the protest which had been raised by Greek philosophers of recognized standing against which they felt that image-worship needed to be defended.

With regard to the Jewish protest we saw that there were two grounds of objection to idolatry—one, the falsity of supposing that an inanimate material thing was alive, that you could give pleasure to any person by what you did to an idol, or get any help yourself from it; two, that to make anything which purported to be a visible similitude of God was to dishonour Him. Both these grounds of protest are found amongst the Greeks long before they came into contact with the Jews. The first is found in the fragment of Heraclitus (round about

Greek Protest Against Idolatry

500 B.C.) which says: "Men pray to these images: this is like trying to converse with the walls of a house."[1] The other ground of objection is found still earlier, in the poem of Xenophanes (sixth century). Those verses of his are almost too familiar to quote, in which he ridicules all conceptions of the deity in human form: if lions and oxen and horses could make images of the gods, they would represent them like lions and oxen and horses: God was a single all-embracing sphere, alive and conscious.

The people who carried on this line of criticism were the Cynics. Amongst the fragments preserved of the founder of the school, Antisthenes, a disciple of Socrates, is one which says that while by popular convention there are many gods, there is in reality (κατὰ φύσιν) only one God. Another runs: "God is not like anybody: no one can learn from an image what He is."

Diogenes of Sinope, the disciple of Antisthenes—the celebrated Diogenes whom legend describes as living in a huge jar—was noted for his refusal to offer any homage to images. Zeno of Citium, the founder of the Stoics (latter part of fourth century B.C.), wrote his early work *On the State* under strong Cynic influence,[2] and a fragment preserved from that affirms that in the ideal city-state, which the book describes, it will not be lawful to build temples: a temple is not a thing worth much, is not holy: "no product of the hands of builders and common craftsmen can have great worth." When the work was quoted by Clement of Alexandria as speci-

[1] Fragment 5.
[2] This early work of Zeno's is frequently quoted as giving the Stoic view of image-worship; but it is questionable how far the Stoics later on would have accepted what their Founder had written before his philosophy had matured.

Holy Images

fically condemning images, as well as temples, he was probably referring to this passage and inserting "images" without warrant in the original text, though it is no doubt true that the condemnation of temples could hardly have any sense apart from the condemnation of images.

There is ground for thinking that the condemnation of image-worship—or, if not condemnation in the stern sense in which idolatry was condemned by Jews and Christians, at any rate the relative depreciation of image-worship, as an unworthy mode of worshipping the deity —was carried on in the last century B.C. by the Platonizing Stoic Posidonius, the encyclopedic and eloquent writer, whose influence is now believed to have been so far-reaching in Greek and Roman philosophy after his time. It is conjectured with some probability that from Posidonius a statement is derived which we find, both in a fragment of Varro quoted by St. Augustine, and in Plutarch's *Life of Numa*. The statement is that the ancient Romans during the first one hundred and seventy years of their history, that is, from the foundation of the city by Romulus to the reign of Tarquinius Priscus, had no representations of the gods in visible form in their religion. They considered it impious, Plutarch adds, for beings of a lower order to make similitudes of their betters: it was impossible to apprehend God otherwise than by inner thought (νοήσει). When Varro reproduced this statement about the one hundred and seventy years, he went on to say: "If the same practice had continued, a purer mode of worship would have been offered to the gods." He pointed to some other religions which had no images—the Jewish amongst them—as examples to be admired. And he ended up by saying: "Those who

Early Romans and Moses

first set up visible representations of the gods for popular worship removed from their peoples a salutary fear and brought in a new error."[1]

Reitzenstein[2] and Heinemann argue for the supposition that the relatively favourable account of Judaism given by Strabo is derived from Posidonius. "Moses," this passage says, "asserted and taught that the Egyptians went astray in judgment when they represented the Divine in the similitude of wild animals or domestic cattle; so did the Libyans; so also did the Greeks with their gods shaped in the likeness of men. The one and only God is this great Whole which embraces us all and the earth and the sea, this to which we give the names 'heaven,' 'kosmos,' *natura rerum*.' What man of any intelligence would dare to make an image of this in the semblance of anything belonging to our lower world? No, all making of images must be eschewed." (It is true, of course, that the description of God here given is Stoic rather than Hebraic.) That God has no locality which men can mark, no face which men can see, that He is to be conceived on the analogy of the invisible mind or soul of man, is an idea we find laid down in passages of Cicero's *Tusculans* which are conjectured also to be derived from Posidonius. It could not therefore have seemed an unnatural corollary that God was best worshipped by inner contemplation. "God is a spirit and they that worship Him must worship Him in spirit" would not have seemed to a contemporary Greek an

---

[1] Augustine, *De Civit. Dei*, iv. 31. Bodo de Borries, *Quid veteres philosophi de idololatria senserint* (Göttingen, 1918).

[2] *Zwei religionsgeschichtliche Fragen*, 1901, p. 77, note. But the view that this passage in Strabo was derived from Posidonius was current long before Reitzenstein wrote: it is accepted as probable by Théodore Reinach in his *Textes relatifs au Judaïsme* (1895), pp. 95, 99.

Holy Images

unfamiliar idea, even if for Jew and Christian the phrase had a content it had not for the Greek.

In the Jewish Book of Wisdom we find a peculiar theory as to the origin of idolatry put forward, which I. Heinemann has maintained to be derived also from Posidonius.[1] His evidence for this is that the same theory is found in Lactantius and in the *Octavius* of Minucius Felix: these Christian writers can be shown to have drawn sometimes from the lost work of Seneca, *De Superstitione*, and Seneca drew from Posidonius. This argument seems to me worth little, in view of the fact that the Book of Wisdom was part of the Bible of Lactantius and Minucius, and it therefore is simpler to suppose that they drew in this case directly from that. The theory is that idolatry had a double origin. One was that a father, when his child died, had an image made of the child in order to fill the desolate void before his eyes, and then instituted a cult to be carried on by a private mystery association in connexion with the image: the other origin was that kings and princes, since they could not be ubiquitous in their dominions, had images of themselves set up to which men could offer homage, and so "flatter the absent as if present." This theory was certainly based upon facts connected with the institution of particular cults which the writer of Wisdom had before his eyes in the Graeco-Roman world of the last century B.C. Private family mystery-cults in which worship was offered to some deceased member of the family are well-known. We have in the case of Cicero an almost exact parallel to the description in the Book of Wisdom; for when his daughter died, he did

[1] Isaak Heinemann, *Poseidonios metaphysische Schriften*, i. pp. 145–148.

The Theory of the Book of Wisdom

try to console himself by deifying her and building a shrine in which ritual homage would be offered her. Again, the Hellenistic kings did promote a worship of themselves offered ritually in different places of their dominions to their images, as a means of securing the loyalty of their subjects, and if the author of Wisdom wrote in Egypt, he would have witnessed such king-worship every day in his own environment. Whether he was right in generalizing from these facts which he saw to the first origin of image-worship among men is another question. So far as I know, the theory is not actually found elsewhere, except in Christian writers who got it from the Book of Wisdom. It may well have been, to start with, the idea of an Alexandrine Jew, contemplating the pagan world, as he saw it around him.

One thing, however, which is interesting, Heinemann does point out in connexion with the view of pagan religion taken in the Book of Wisdom—the relatively mild judgment passed on the worship of the heavenly bodies and other natural phenomena, as compared with the homage offered to images made by men.

> "For these men there is but small blame,
> For they too peradventure do but go astray
> While they are seeking God and desiring to find him.
> For living among his works they make diligent search
> And they yield themselves up to sight, because the things that they look upon are beautiful."
>
> (xiii. 6, 7.)

Heinemann points out that this relatively mild judgment of the worship of natural objects was quite un-Jewish: for the Old Testament and for Rabbinic Judaism, worship of the sun and moon was just as abominable

Holy Images

as idolatry; but a judgment similar to that of Wisdom is found, Heinemann shows, in Philo: "All those who are votaries and worshippers of the sun and the moon, of the whole sky and the kosmos and the most perfect parts therein, as if they were gods, go astray indeed—there can be no question of that—exalting the subjects above the sovereign, but their wrong-doing is not so heinous as that of the others, the makers of images."[1]

It may well be that both these Hellenistic Jewish writers were influenced in this matter by popular Stoicism. If Posidonius had condemned image-worship as an aberration and contrasted with it a purer and more ancient worship which was directed to the manifestation of God in nature, contemplating especially the sky and the shining bodies moving therein in wondrous order—shining bodies which were alive and conscious—it may well be that this had led Hellenistic Jews to make a distinction in grade of evil between star-worship and image-worship. The source, as we saw, from which Strabo got his account of the original religion of Moses—which may have been Posidonius—seemed to identify God with the sky. And Philo, while he, of course, thought worship of the heavenly bodies wrong, a worship of creatures instead of the Creator, himself shared, we know as a fact, the current view of the Greek world that the heavenly bodies were alive and conscious.[2]

When we now turn back to the defence of image-worship offered by Dio Chrysostom and Maximus of

[1] *De Decalogo*, 66.
[2] Every region of the universe, Philo has said, has its proper inhabitants: the sky has the stars. καὶ γὰρ οὗτοι ψυχαὶ ὅλαι δι' ὅλων ἀκήρατοί τε καὶ θεῖαι, παρὸ καὶ κύκλῳ κινοῦνται τὴν συγγενεστάτην νῷ κίνησιν· νοῦς γὰρ ἕκαστος αὐτῶν ἀκραιφνέστατος, *De Gigantibus*, § 8 (Cohn-Windland, II. 43).

Dio's Defence of Images

Tyre, we see that there really were adverse criticisms current of old in the Greek world which they had to meet.

Both Dio and Maximus defend image-worship as a concession to the weakness of human nature. The idea that the image is identical with the deity, or that the deity actually resides in the image, never comes into consideration. Neither is the idea that the deity has any bodily form which the image resembles entertained as possible. To worship God in spirit, Maximus recognizes, to elevate the mind to Him without the mediation of any visible image, is the highest and best worship. But there are few people, he says, capable of it.[1] Dio describes[2] how the idea of God is originally begotten in man by the majestic spectacle of the universe. In some of the forms of initiation into the mysteries the person being initiated was set upon a throne, and, without anything being explained to him in words, he witnessed the performance all round him of an imposing ritual, solemn music and dancing. The spectacle alone subjugated his soul. We, Dio says, are situated, not, as such a neophyte is, in a little chamber, but in the immense environment whose every part declares the glory of God, night and day performing their ordered dance around us continually. The first fathers of the human race were nearer akin to the Divine than we are. They had before their eyes many witnesses of the truth (God had left not Himself without *witness*, St. Paul had written two generations before—the same word), witnesses which suffered them not to sink into stupor or go their way unheeding, the world shining all round about them with divine and

---
[1] Maximus Tyrius, II. 2.
[2] Dio Chrys., Oration xii, *De Dei Cognitione*.

Holy Images

mighty sights, sky and stars, sun and moon, manifold voices of winds and woods and rivers and sea. There was the marvellous provision in nature for human needs, earth and air together like fostering mothers, offering nourishment, supplying breath. The order and regularity of Nature itself testifies of God. Even the plants by some sort of dim instinct obey the law and bring forth their proper fruit in season. And this dim instinct of obedience running through the world of plants and animals is a better wisdom than the perverted reason of people like the Epicureans, who think of the gods as marooned far away somewhere in the spaces between the worlds, and do not believe the world movement even to have been started by any rational power, not even to be like the movement of a child's hoop, which, if it is allowed to run by itself, was at any rate started by the child.

All this, of course, is the regular Stoic theology, the stock argument from teleological adaptation and order in nature. The God whom it presents is as far as possible from being anthropomorphic in bodily shape. He is the unseen Wisdom, Ruler, Pilot, behind the immense universe. Why then should any image of Him in human shape be made? Would it not be enough to look up at the night sky with its ordered multitude of moving lights, each one a living, conscious divinity, and adore the Divine there? Dio says that it would not be enough. There is one thing which all such worship of God in His sublime transcendence lacks—the sense of intimate nearness, the satisfaction of the human craving to touch. That may be a weakness in human nature; but there it is. Pathetic it may well be deemed, as when little children, Dio says, reach out in the dark to make sure that mother is really there, to feel her close to them. Images are the

Phidias and Homer

only way man has for satisfying this exigence: the great God in the sky is very far away. But the image can be seen and touched. Of course it is only a symbol, but it seems to bring God nearer. As a symbol, it must, of course, be quite inadequate as a representation of the reality; but an image in human form, Dio thinks, is the least inadequate symbol possible for men. For Dio believes that man is in some respects more like God than any other visible being on earth. His view of God would be open to the same charge of anthropomorphism as is brought against any view of God as personal. God has not a body like man's body, but man's soul is, in the Stoic view, of the same nature as God. If that is so, the best symbol of God may well be considered an image in human form, for the human form is, among all visible things on earth, the vehicle and index of the soul. And so far as the Zeus of Phidias at Olympia seems to express certain qualities of soul, the symbol does resemble the reality. Its suggestion of majesty and power conveys the idea of something which is really true of God, that which we indicate when we speak of God as Ruler and King; its graciousness and benignity suggest that in God which we indicate when we speak of Him as Father; its gravity and austerity that which we indicate when we speak of Him as the Father of Law in societies of men. Dio enforces his argument by urging that whether you have graven and painted images or not, you cannot get away from imaginative symbolism in your thought of God. The descriptions of Zeus in Homer create the mental picture of someone in glorified human form which is in effect similar to the image given by a representation in wood or stone. If Phidias is to be condemned for carving his image, you must condemn Homer too.

Holy Images

About a century after Dio wrote his oration, the defence of images was taken up by Porphyry in an early work, the treatise *About Images* (Περὶ 'Αγαλμάτων) at a time when the old paganism was feeling the pressure of the Christian attack.[1] It is only the uneducated, Porphyry says, who identify the gods with the images. The images are to be taken purely as symbols, both as regards their material, their colour, and their form. White marble typifies the quality of light in the gods, gold their stainlessness, and so on. Zeus is represented as a man, because man is the rational being and Zeus had ordered the world by reason. He is represented sitting, to show the stability of his power. His upper part is bare and his lower part mantled, to show that he is manifested to the intelligences of heaven, but hidden for those of the lower sphere. He holds his sceptre in his left hand, because the heart is on the left side, the heart (according to the Stoics) the seat of the Ruling Mind in man, and the world is ruled by Mind. He holds out in his right hand either an eagle to show that he is lord of the powers of the air, as the eagle is the king of the birds, or a figure of Victory to show that he is supreme over all. And so on with the traditional representations of the other gods. In Porphyry's *apologia* for images two things may be noted. (1) It is not a question of image-*worship*. Porphyry says nothing about the direction of homage or sacrifice to the images; it is not what men do to the images that comes into consideration, but what the images do to man. They serve, by the way of symbolism, to bring home to the mind of the man who contemplates them, various characteristics of the Divine Power.

---
[1] The remaining fragments of this work may be found collected in J. Bidez, *Vie de Porphyre* (1913).

Porphyry on Images

(2) The Divine Power is here thought of on Stoic, rather than on Neoplatonic, lines, as the Power working in physical nature, in the movement of the heavenly bodies, the sun and moon, the waters upon earth, animal reproduction and vegetation. The ithyphallic figure of Hermes typifies the spermatic *logos* permeating the universe. It is really all one Power, encompassing the earth (περίγειος) and to this man's worship is directed (θρησκευέται), but in its different activities it is represented by different gods and goddesses—as fashioning rocks and stones, by Rhea; as producing green vegetable things, by Demeter; as inspiring oracles, by Themis; as penetrated by the spermatic *logos*, by Priapus; as quickening dry seeds, by Korē; as the life of plants beginning to sprout in the ground, by Dionysus; as undergoing the assaults which the blossom has to undergo, by Attis; as the growth cut down in its maturity, by Adonis. Spiritually, this treatise of Porphyry's is on a much lower level than Dio's oration, or than the Neoplatonism which Porphyry afterwards learnt from Plotinus. We shall see that in a writing of his later life, when Porphyry was steeped in Neoplatonism, he speaks of the worship of images with relative depreciation, and that in yet another writing he accepted the view that the beings to whom animal sacrifice was offered—the beings, that is, inhabiting the images—were daemons of inferior character. Porphyry's beliefs varied at different periods of his life.

In the writings of Porphyry's master, Plotinus, which Porphyry edited, another theory of the purpose of an image is adumbrated, a theory making the image much more than a mere symbol which brings a certain truth about the universe to the mind of him who looks at it.

Holy Images

What Plotinus indeed does is to build on the popular view which makes the deity actually come to inhabit the image and give a refined philosophic version of it. The purpose of an image is to enable the worshipper to come into real contact with the World Soul. Of course, the World Soul cannot be supposed to come down itself into the bit of matter constituting the image (κατελθεῖν εἰς τοῦτο). Yet particular material things have a quality which attracts the World Soul by a kind of sympathy. And one thing which gives a material thing such a quality is its being a likeness or "in some way an imitation (ὁπωσοῦν μιμηθέν)" of the Soul. It is then analogous to a mirror which captures the form of a visible object (ἁρπάσαι εἶδός τι δυνάμενον) although the visible object does not itself enter into the mirror. Thus the image can receive a certain part or apportionment of the World Soul (ὑποδέξασθαι δυνάμενον μοῖράν τινα αὐτῆς). The World Soul in its higher existence remains in the intelligential world, attached inseparably to *Nous*, but in its lower part it "as it were" goes forth from *Nous* to inform the material world (τῇ οἷον ἀπελθούσῃ ψυχῇ), and since the image, by its having resemblance to something in the World Soul, draws to itself an extra portion of the Soul, a man by means of the image can come into communion with the Higher Soul and with the *Nous* to which the Higher Soul is always directed.[1]

---

[1] Enneads iv. 11. 3. The translation of E. Bréhier in the Budé edition of Plotinus seems to me to make nonsense of one sentence, τῇ μὲν ἐξ ἀρχῆς ψυχῇ προσηρτῆσθαι τῇ οἷον ἀπελθούσῃ ψυχῇ. He takes the second ψυχῇ to be in apposition to the first—"*ils sont liés à l'âme primitive, à celle qui sort en quelque sorte de l'intelligence.*" But the ἐξ ἀρχῆς ψυχή is surely contrasted with the οἷον ἀπελθοῦσα ψυχή, and the second dative is instrumental. "They are attached to the original Soul by means of the Soul which has come forth."

The Theory of Plotinus

This theory of the sympathy by which certain kinds or forms of matter attract the Higher Powers or particular Beings belonging to the higher region, underlay, of course, the system of "theurgy" which was so important a part of the later baser Neoplatonism represented by Iamblichus. It is expounded in a passage of the work *De Mysteriis*, which is probably by Iamblichus himself, or, if not, belongs to the same type of Neoplatonic theosophy.[1]

This furnished a "scientific theology" (the *De Mysteriis* talks of ἐπιστημονικὴ θεολογία!) which justified the image-worship of the old religion, the philosophic view shading off insensibly into the more literally realistic view, according to which, as we have seen, the material image was actually indwelt by a god or daemon.

Of the two objections brought against image-worship —that it treats a lifeless material thing as alive, that the image professes to offer a portrait of God—it is obvious that neither the first nor the second has any application to image-worship as conceived by Dio. The question he raises is whether the use of images in human form is legitimate, as representations of the really existing object or objects of worship. This was the same question which confronted Christians when they had to consider, not pagan idolatry—that they condemned on both the grounds already specified, as well as on a third ground to which we shall come—but image-worship within the Christian Church.

In our next lecture, we shall deal with the question of image-worship in the Christian Church, but before we pass to that, in the conclusion of this lecture, we may

[1] A translation of this passage may be found in my *Later Greek Religion* (Dent, 1927), pp. 225, 226.

Holy Images

notice what seem traces of two subsidiary feelings determining amongst Greeks or Jews an opposition to image-worship or the making of images. One feeling is that the connexion of human manual work with something so holy as an image which is to represent the divine is to be eschewed. The root of this feeling might, amongst the Greeks, be conjectured to be the feeling that manual work was itself ignoble, the feeling which put manual workers as a whole in the class of the *banausoi*. It may be remembered that when Zeno, the founder of Stoicism, in his early work on the Republic, declared that in the ideal City there would be no temples, it was on the ground that "no product of the hands of builders and common craftsmen can have great worth."[1]

Another root of the feeling might be the idea of something holy as essentially that which it was dangerous or wrong to touch. True, the image, while it was being manufactured, was not yet anything holy: nevertheless, it was destined to be the abode or the vehicle of a god, and to think of human hands making so free with it as they would in the workman's shop may have been repugnant. At any rate, there seems ground for believing that, for one reason or another, the manufacture of the idol by the hands of men was sometimes felt to be an unfortunate derogation to its dignity. Such a feeling explains the special regard paid to images which were believed to have fallen from heaven. The most generally-known case is, of course, the image of Artemis at Ephesus, mentioned in the Book of the Acts. Some of these images, like that of the Great Mother, transported

---

[1] Compare Seneca (quoted by Augustine, *De Civ. Dei*, vi. 10), "Sacros immortales inviolabiles in materia vilissima atque immobili dedicant."

Images Not Made by Hands

from Pessinus in Asia Minor to Rome, were not really images at all but unshaped stones, perhaps meteorites which had in one sense literally fallen from heaven. Others apparently were images really fashioned by men, to which a legend had become attached, whether by priestly fraud or by popular fancy, representing them as things with a divine, not a human, origin.

Rationalist sceptics in the Greek world apparently felt that it required explanation how, if an image was really made by men, it can have been given out to the people that it was of divine origin, for the workmen who had been engaged on its manufacture and transport would be there to testify to the contrary. The most likely answer to the difficulty is, of course, that the belief in the divine origin of an image did not arise till many generations after the image had been set up in the temple when its real origin was forgotten. Greek rationalist stories, on the other hand, told how, when images were set up which were to be passed off as not made by human hands, the artists and workmen employed upon them were killed before they had opportunity to expose the fraud. A story of this kind was repeated by the Christian writer Isidore of Pelusium, about an image of Artemis set up by one of the Ptolemies at Alexandria. As soon as the image was in place, Ptolemy invited all concerned in its manufacture, the story says, to a great dinner at the bottom of a pit, and then had the pit filled in, during the dinner, and all the guests buried alive.[1] The story is of rather poor invention: an invitation to a dinner at the bottom of a pit is one sufficiently strange to make some receivers of it, one would think, hold back: also

[1] Isidorus of Pelusium, *Epistles*, iv. 207. (Migne, *Tom.* lxxviii, col. 1300.)

Holy Images

the story only removes the difficulty a degree farther back: it gets rid of the workmen who made the image, but it leaves us with the workmen who must have been employed to fill in the pit. The story, however, shows that a need was felt for a rationalist explanation of the legends which declared certain images not to have been made by any human hands. If the critical theory, alluded to in our last lecture, regarding the prohibition of image-worship in ancient Israel, is true—that there was a time when a graven image was considered wrong and a molten image inoffensive, because the hands of men had been occupied upon a graven image in a way they had not been occupied upon a molten image—then we should have amongst the Israelites also the trace of an analogous feeling to the one just indicated amongst the Greeks.

A second feeling which may have contributed to the conviction that it was wrong to make an image is that an image or picture is a false pretence. It has an appearance of being a man or an animal, but is not; it is an acted lie. We should perhaps hardly have thought that such an idea could arise in the minds of men, were it not that it seems to be the chief ground on which the objection to making representations of living things is based in Islam. It is wrong, according to Moslem doctrine, to make the picture of a fish because you cannot make a live fish. It is difficult for us to follow the logical process involved. There is no *deception*, we might say: the picture does not pretend to be more than a picture. That does not justify it: the fact remains that the picture is not true: the thing there that you have made to look like a fish is not a fish. The only way, perhaps, by which we can at all come to understand such reasoning, is to think of the analogous disapproval, in some old-fashioned

All Fiction to be Condemned

Puritan or Evangelical circles, of fictitious stories. A novel was thought wrong, not only because it might incidentally contain suggestions which were vicious, but by its very character as the narrative of something which never really happened. Here, too, it might be said, there was no deception: it did not profess to be more than a story. The defence was not admitted: it was fiction, falsehood; that was enough. I remember in my childhood reading an Evangelical pamphlet on the wickedness of any kind of fiction. The title of the pamphlet was "Is it true?" In the course of the argument, the writer encountered the objection that the *Iliad* and *Odyssey* were fiction, and yet it was considered right for boys to study the *Iliad* and *Odyssey* at school. He decided that in this case the fictitious character of the narrative might be overlooked because a study of the *Iliad* and *Odyssey*, which were in Greek, might be serviceable for a better understanding of the New Testament. You seem here to have a close analogy to the Moslem feeling that the picture of a fish must be wrong because it is not a real fish. At the Day of Judgment, if you have painted the picture of a fish, some scholars in Islam have said, you will be confronted with it, and God will require you to make it alive. You will look at the false appearance which you made once in an inconsiderate moment; you will look helplessly, knowing that no power of yours can make the wretched thing come to life; and God will condemn you to hell.[1]

It is, of course, true that the prohibition against making pictures of living things has not been strictly observed in Islam. Persian art, as has been brought home to us

[1] E. W. Lane, *Manners and Customs of the Modern Egyptians*, ch. iii. (fifth edition, 1871, vol. i. p. 120).

Holy Images

by a recent exhibition in London, was rich in its representations of men and animals, though, of course, the Persians are Shiites, heretics according to the majority of Moslems. To-day, in Moslem countries generally, the prohibition against making pictures and images has become a dead letter: in Cairo, the seat of the great Sunni University, statues adorn the public streets as they might those of any European town. In former times some Moslem theologians in those parts of the world where pictures were commonly made sought a way of reconciling practice with the prescriptions of the religion. The religion forbade making the picture of any *living* thing, and the theologians decided that if, in the picture of a man or a horse, there was a line drawn across the neck (as in most pictures there would naturally be, the top edge of the clothes or the horse's harness), such a line might be considered to decapitate the man or the animal, and so cause them to count as dead—even though the picture might represent a scene in which men and horses were engaged in the most violent activities of life.

Were it not that this idea—the wrongness of making a picture because it is a pretence—were found so pronounced in Islam, one would hardly look for traces of it in earlier traditions. Among the Greeks it is indeed inconceivable. The only approach to it is, perhaps, the idea in Plato's *Republic* that the picture of a bed is removed a step further from truth than an actual particular bed. The particular bed is, of course, less true that the ideal Bed, and the picture of a bed is a remove still further away. One could not say that there was any suggestion that it was *wrong* to make the picture of a bed: still the degrees of nearness to truth do seem to imply, in Plato's thought, degrees of value, so that you have perhaps here

Art Trenches on God's Prerogative

a relative depreciation of the representation of things in art as compared with the things themselves. It might suggest that to be occupied with the making of images of things was to direct yourself to an unworthy play with illusion and vanity.

In Rabbinical literature there is a passage which, in view of the Moslem idea, may be thought to contain the germ of it. Rabbi Joshua ben Levi (about A.D. 250) said: "Come and see how God's way differs from man's way. Man paints a picture on a wall, but he can put therein no spirit, no soul, no viscera. Not so God: He fashions one form within another form (i.e. the child within the mother) and He puts therein spirit and soul and viscera. That is what Hannah said: 'There is none holy as the Lord, for there is none beside thee: neither is there any'—"Rock," the Hebrew word means, but by pointing it differently the Rabbi could make it mean "Designer" or "Fashioner"—'like our God.'"[1] It is not far from this to the Moslem idea that by making the image or picture of a living thing you fashion a false appearance which trenches upon the prerogative of the Creator. But if this idea existed in germ in Judaism, it was quite subordinate. There is a trace of it, perhaps, in some of the early Christian utterances against idolatry to which we shall come next time.

[1] *Berakhoth* 10a.

LECTURE III

The Christian Church arose in a world given to idolatry, but arose out of the Jewish community which maintained, in the midst of that world, its intransigent protest against image-worship.[1] When the new community of those who believed in Jesus became loosed from its original Jewish connexions, when it consisted mainly of those drawn in from the pagan world, it abandoned much of the Jewish tradition—Sabbaths and circumcision and the distinction between clean and unclean meats, and it adopted a number of things from its Greek environment —"baptized" them into its own system, in Professor Percy Gardner's phrase. From the point of view of an unconverted pagan, the Christians seemed to retain a great deal of irrational Jewish prejudice; from the point of view of Jews they seemed to be assimilated to the sinners, the Gentiles. At the outset the image-worship which the Christians had to consider was the pagan worship of many gods. With regard to that, the Christians continued the Jewish protest with undiminished emphasis. Then, if we look on seven centuries, when the Roman Empire has long been professedly Christian and pagan idolatry in the Mediterranean countries is a thing of the past, we see the Christian Church making images and

[1] I must acknowledge, in treating the early Christian attitude to image-worship, my special obligation to three monographs: H. Koch, *Die altchristliche Bildfrage nach den literarischen Quellen* (1917); W. Elliger, *Die Stellung der alten Christen zu den Bildern in den ersten vier Jahrhunderten* (Leipzig, 1930), *Zur Enstehung und frühen Entwicklung der altchristlichen Bildkunst* (Leipzig, 1934).

Early Church and Pagan Idolatry

pictures to which it offers religious homage as freely as the pagans had done to the images of their gods. But we find also a protest against this image-worship raised in the Christian Church itself, the charge brought by a section of the Church that Christian image-worship is so similar to the old pagan image-worship, as to come, like that, under the category of idolatry, and, from the side of the Church, an answer made which seeks to draw a sharp line of distinction between this image-worship and that, to show that one is rightly called idolatry and the other not. Here the abandonment of the old Jewish code, the adoption—can we say baptism?—of something that looks very like the practice of the old pagan environment is conspicuous. That is the remarkable sequence of things which we have to study.

To take first the protest made by the Christian Church in its early days against the pagan idolatry of its environment; while that protest was largely a continuation of the Jewish protest on the same lines, there were two ways in which we may perhaps see a difference between the Christian protest and the Jewish. The Jewish protest, as we saw, condemned not only the offering of homage to images, but the very making of images or pictures of certain things. There is, I believe, no clear statement in an early Christian Father that it is wrong to make the image or picture of any class of objects—living creatures or human beings or any of the other things which it had been forbidden in the Jewish community, at one time or another, to portray. When Tertullian insists that it is not only the worship of an idol which has been forbidden by God in the Mosaic Law but the making of an idol,[1] one could not infer certainly from such a sentence that

[1] *Idolum tam fieri quam coli Deus prohibet. De Idol.,* 4.

Holy Images

Tertullian regarded it as wrong to make the representation of a man which was not intended to be worshipped: he speaks of the making of an *idol*. Yet it seems probable that the profession of a sculptor or painter was commonly regarded in the Church as one which a Christian could not consistently follow: the legend which made St. Luke a painter had not yet been invented. When Tertullian, in reference to the prohibition in the Second Commandment, the prohibition to make the similitude of any object in heaven or on earth or in the water, says that "for the servants of God the whole expanse of the Universe is thus excluded for the purposes of such an art,"[1] he may really mean to express a view not far from the Jewish one. In some of the early Church Orders there are regulations that point in the same direction. "No oblations may be received from those who paint with colours, from those who make idols or workers in gold, silver and bronze."[2] In a pseudo-Clementine Church Order, a painter (ζωγράφος) is put in the same list with a harlot, a brothel-keeper, a drunkard, an actor, and an athlete.[3] But it is possible that in all these cases it is understood that by painter is meant the painter of idolatrous pictures. In the Egyptian Didascalia this is clear: "If any one is a sculptor or a painter, let him be instructed not to make idols: he must either cease from doing so or be expelled from the church."

In the two Fathers of the Alexandrine School, Clement and Origen, one may see the trace of a feeling alluded to in our last lecture—that the representation of objects in

[1] *Toto mundo eiusmodi artibus interdixit servis Dei. De Idol.*, 4.
[2] The Syriac Didascalia (third century), German translation by H. Achelis and J. Fleming (*Texte u. Untersuchungen zur Gesch. d. altchrist. Literatur. Neue Folge*, vol. x, Leipzig, 1904), chapter xviii.
[3] A. P. de Lagarde, *Reliq. jur. eccl. antiq.*, 1856, p. 87.

Clement of Alexandria

art is something unworthy because it is not true. Here the influence of Platonism comes in, the depreciation of sense-perception, of τὰ αἰσθητά, as compared with intellectual apprehension, of ὕλη as compared with eternal reality. Visible man, Clement says, is himself only an image of God. "But an image of the image, the statues made in the likeness of men and far removed from the truth, appear only as a fleeting impression. I could see therefore little but madness in a life which was occupied so earnestly with matter"—the life, Clement means, of the sculptor or painter.[1] Clement cannot even believe that where the Pentateuch speaks of Moses having had images of Cherubim made for the Tabernacle, we are to understand the text literally. The term Cherub must be a symbolical way of referring to the rational soul; there is no creature in heaven with a shape capable of being sensibly perceived such as a Cherub would be, literally understood. "It is unthinkable that he who forbade the making of any graven image (Moses) would himself have made a representation in human form of the holy beings."[2]

In one passage it is odd to find Clement condemning images and pictures, not on the ground that they break the Second Commandment, but that they break the Eighth: "Thou shalt not steal"! "The artist would rob God: he seeks to usurp the Divine prerogative of creation and by means of his plastic or graphic art, pretends to be a maker of animals and plants."[3] Plants, even, notice, may not be portrayed. This goes further than the Moslem prohibition. Otherwise this passage is a remarkable anticipation of the Moslem view.

When Origen draws a picture of the polity of Israel as the ideal Republic, he says that in that State there was

[1] *Protrept.*, x. 98. 3. [2] *Stromata* v. 36. 44. [3] *Stromata* vi. 16. 147.

Holy Images

neither painter nor statuary: "all such persons the Law cast out from it, so that there might be no pretext for that making of images, a thing which attracts the foolish among men and draws the eyes of the soul down from God to earth."[1] The Law, he says, desired that men should be occupied with the *reality* in the case of each object, should not fabricate things which were other than the truth (ἕτερα παρὰ τὴν ἀλήθειαν), which mendaciously assumed the appearance of male or female sex or of being birds or beasts or fishes.

Clement, indeed, in one passage makes a concession in regard to the designs on signet-rings worn by Christians: he suggests not only the representation of inanimate things—a ship, a lyre, an anchor—but even that of a dove or a fish. It seems unlikely that he would have allowed a human figure.

In this belief, that a picture or image was wrong because it was not true, Tertullian is at one with the two Alexandrine Fathers. "If you come to the make-believe of the theatres," he says (*opus personarum*), "I very much doubt whether it is pleasing to God. God forbids the making of any similitude. How much more does He forbid the making of a similitude of His own image, man! The author of truth loves not falsehood: everything fictitious is in His eyes adultery."[2]

So far as the dislike of pictures and images was influenced by the Platonic depreciation of sensible perception in comparison with intellectual apprehension it is true, of course, that from Plato himself substantial justification could have been derived for regarding a sensible object as a stepping-stone to higher things, man might mount by the ladder of visible beauty to intellectual beauty.

[1] *C. Celsus* iv. 31.   [2] *De spectac.*, 23.

Origen and Tatian

This brings us again to the very crux of symbolism which we meet over and over again throughout these lectures. The symbol may be an indispensable help so long as you mount beyond it to the thing symbolized; but it is a snare so far as you are caught in it and prevented from rising. When Plato talks of the visible beauty as directing men to the intellectual beauty he is thinking of the symbol in regard to the former possibility; when Origen speaks of works of art as drawing "the eyes of the soul from God to earth" he is thinking of the symbol in regard to the latter possibility.

In Tatian, who represents, it is true, an anti-Hellenic bitterness and an asceticism not characteristic of the Church as a whole—though it is combined, curiously, with a pleasure in the display of Greek rhetoric—we get a general attack on Greek art—sculpture and painting. Tatian, however, attacks it, not on the ground that art is essentially false make-believe, but because of its choice of subjects. He gives a list of the women of evil repute whom the Greek world had honoured by statues. Side by side with the celebrated courtesans, it is odd to find one woman whose only offence in Tatian's eyes was apparently that she had had thirty children.[1] It has to be remembered that Tatian belonged to the heretical sect of Encratites who disapproved of marriage.

In spite, however, of these approximations in early Christian writers to the Jewish view, it remains, I think, true that there is no clear statement in any early Christian writing to the effect that it is definitely wrong to make the

[1] Τί μοι διὰ τὸ Περικλύμενον γύναιον, ὅπερ ἐκύησε τριάκοντα παῖδας, ὡς θαυμαστὸν ἡγεῖσθε καὶ κατανοεῖν ποίημα; πολλῆς γὰρ ἀκρασίας ἀπενεγκαμένην τὰ ἀκροθίνια βδελύττεσθαι καλὸν ἦν, τῇ κατὰ Ῥωμαίους συῒ παρεικαζομένην, ἥτις καὶ αὐτὴ διὰ τὸ ὅμοιον μυστικωτέρας ἠξίωται θεραπείας (Oratio ad Graecos, 34).

Holy Images

representation of a living creature, or of a human being, even when there is no question of worshipping it.

The second way in which the early Christian attack on pagan idolatry differs from the Jewish is that the Christians took much more seriously the pagan claim that the images were animated by spirits. Yes, the Christian writers say, there *are* spirits in the idols: the spirits are devils.

The idea that the gods of the nations are evil spirits is found in the Old Testament. "They sacrificed," it says in Deuteronomy xxxii. 17, "to devils (*shēdhīm*) and not to God." Or again in Psalm cvi. 37: "They sacrificed their sons and daughters to devils." In Leviticus xvii. 7, another word is used, though equally translated "devils" in our Bibles: They shall no more offer their sacrifices to *s'īrīm*, "hairy creatures," a word our Bibles elsewhere translate "satyrs" when used of the beings who dance and howl in lonely places. But there is not in the Old Testament any close association of a particular evil spirit with a particular idol: idol-worshippers are ridiculed in the passages quoted in a former lecture as offering homage to mere wood and stone: it is implied that there is no personality at all there.

These latter passages formed part of the Bible of the early Christians and were no doubt commonly applied by them to the idolatry of the surrounding Greek world. They were not really consistent with the view that the images were animated by devils. But Christians were probably not conscious of any inconsistency. We find St. Paul saying in one passage (1 Cor. viii. 4): "We know that no idol is anything in the world, and that there is no god but one," and in another passage soon after (x. 19, 20): "What say I then? That a thing sacrificed to idols is

Devils in the Idols

anything, or that an idol is anything? But I say that the things which the Gentiles sacrifice they sacrifice to devils, and not to God; and I would not that ye should have communion with devils."

From Plato onwards the ancient pagan world believed in a class of daemons intermediate between gods and men, inhabiting the air between earth and the uppermost heaven. In Plutarch we find the idea that these daemons are not only inferior in nature to the gods but may be morally on a low level: an interlocutor in one of his dialogues explains the unedifying stories told about gods in Greek mythology on the theory that the beings to whom they applied were daemons, not gods.[1] Not all daemons were evil; there are differences of good and bad amongst them, as amongst men. This view was a regular part of the tradition derived from the Platonic Academy; it goes on with richer elaboration in Neoplatonism. Porphyry in the latter part of the third century A.D. gives a systematic account of the maleficent daemons, distinguished from the good daemons. It is the maleficent daemons who inflict plagues, sterility, earthquakes, drought, upon men. But, further, it is the inferior daemons who delight in the reek of animal sacrifice. It may be prudent, Porphyry says, for cities which desire material good things to offer sacrifice to the inferior daemons: even philosophers, like himself, would do so, only taking care to set their hearts not upon the material goods which these daemons could give, but upon the higher good, assimilation in spirit to the Supreme God.[2]

But a century and a half before Porphyry the same thing

---

[1] *On the Cessation of Oracles*, 10–17.
[2] *De Abstinentia*, ii. 43. A translation of the passage may be found in my *Later Greek Religion* (Dent).

Holy Images

had been clearly stated by Celsus in his book against the Christians. There were daemons of low, earthly propensities who were attracted by the fat and blood of the sacrifices, and if men worship them, they should take care, Celsus said, not to draw in the quality of these lower spirits, not to become lovers of the body and forgetful of higher things.[1] The view must have been a common one amongst philosophic pagans in those centuries.

It will be seen that the Christians, when they attacked pagan idolatry as devil-worship, had to do little except use the weapons the pagans themselves put into their hands. When they said that inside the idol was a devil who took pleasure in the fumes of sacrifice they were really saying little more than was implied in Neoplatonist teachings about some images, at any rate. It is true that there were differences. The pagans used the word *daemon* to mean an invisible being of air, inferior to the gods, who might be good as well as bad: the Christians used the word *daemon*—or its diminutive *daimonion*—to mean one of a class of beings all of whom were bad, and whereas with the pagans even a bad daemon was thought to be only morally imperfect, not evil through and through, with the Christians *daimonia* were pure evil, what we understand by the word *devils*.

So far as the Christians believed that inside the idol there really was an evil spirit who delighted in the fumes of sacrifice, they could not, as was said just now, consistently use the mockery of image-worship they found in their Bibles. When you offered the sacrifice of an animal with its mess of blood and stench to an idol, you were not ridiculously trying to gratify a thing of mere wood

[1] Origen. *C. Celsus* viii. 60.

Sacrifice Gratifies Devils

and stone; you were giving keen sensual enjoyment to a devil. The daemons who are occupied with matter are, Athenagoras says,[1] "greedy for the reek of sacrifice and the blood of victims." We took note in a former lecture of a pagan philosopher who had a gift of clairvoyance by which he could detect whether an image was alive or not. Similarly, a Christian writer (Tatian) tells us that the bodies of daemons, being made of fire and air, are invisible to the ordinary man, to ψυχικοί, but can be easily perceived by those who are kept by the spirit of God.[2] Further the pagans are right, not only when they think that sacrifice offered to an idol can gratify a spirit, but when they believe that spirits can act, give counsel or perform miracles through the images. "The impure spirits," says the Christian interlocutor in Minucius Felix, "hide themselves in the statues and consecrated images, and by the afflatus they give forth acquire with men the authority of a present deity, inspiring soothsayers, haunting temples, uttering oracles."[3] The miracles which, according to the pagans, had been wrought by certain images—miracles of healing and so on—some Christian writers allow to have been real miracles wrought by devils.

According to the theory put forward most clearly by Euhemerus, the deities worshipped by the Greeks had been simply men of note in the past who had been deified by a fiction, as Alexander the Great was deified. This theory, which pious pagans regarded as impious rationalism, was eagerly taken up by Jews and Christians. We

[1] *Libellus pro Christianis*, 27.
[2] Τοῖς Πνεύματι Θεοῦ φρουρουμένοις εὐσύνοπτα καὶ τὰ τῶν δαιμονίων ἐστι σώματα. (*Oratio ad Graecos*, 15.)
[3] *Octavius*, 27.

Holy Images

find in Athenagoras the attempt to combine it with the theory that the spirits behind the idols were devils. The combination was made by supposing that Zeus, Apollo, Hermes, and so on, had been real men, as Euhemerus asserted, and the mythological stories attached to them were based upon their real exploits. But the spirits who obtained sensual gratification through sacrifice offered to the images of Zeus, Apollo, and Hermes, who gave oracles, or performed miracles through the images, were not really Zeus, Apollo, and Hermes. They were devils who had falsely assumed the names of those dead men and pretended to be those men—just as the prevalent Catholic theory of Spiritualism to-day asserts that there are real spirits who communicate through tables or automatic writing, but they are not the dead persons whom they pretend to be; they are evil spirits who impersonate them. Athenagoras speaks of one man, Neryllinus, who had died only a short while before, but whose image now did miracles of healing. It was a devil who had seized the opportunity to substitute himself for the spirit of the dead man.[1]

Side by side with this view of pagan image-worship, we find also expressions of the other view, that the idols are mere matter—ἄψυχα καὶ νεκρά, inanimate and dead in Justin's phrase,[2] and Clement of Alexandria seems expressly to repudiate the view that an idol was the habitation of a daemon. "Those who make gods," he says, "do not, according to my view (κατά γε αἴσθησιν τὴν ἐμήν) worship gods and daemons, but mere earth and human art, for that is what the images are (γῆν καὶ τέχνην).[3] Yet Clement certainly believed that the pagan gods were unclean spirits, who sometimes showed them-

[1] *Libellus pro Christianis*, 26.   [2] *Apol.*, 9.   [3] *Protrept.*, iv. 51.

Devils in Disguise

selves to men in the form of ghosts (σκιοειδῆ φαντάσματα).[1]

The emphasis given in the Christian polemic against idolatry to the identification of the pagan gods with devils has an important bearing on the later development —the adoption of image-worship in the Christian Church. For, by identifying the gods with devils, the emphasis of the polemic against idolatry was put upon the objects of worship rather than upon the mode of worship. The objection was now not so much that use was made of an image, as that the worship was directed to an evil power. Later on it was important, as we shall see, for the defenders of image-worship amongst the Christians to make as plain as they could the distinction between their image-worship and pagan idolatry. Looked at from the outside, the forms of worship in the two cases showed remarkable similarity: Christians felt that they could establish the difference by insisting that the objects of worship were so different, that Jesus and His Mother, the Christian saints and martyrs, were not to be compared to the devils who had masked themselves as Apollo or Hermes or Athena or Aphrodite. Thus the theory which made the pagan gods devils in disguise helped to clear the way for image-worship in the Christian Church.

It is to this, the use of images for religious purposes in the Christian Church, that we now come. That in the eighth century the practice of image-worship was general in the Christian Church both east and west, is, of course, recognized by everybody. But in regard to the early centuries there is to-day considerable controversy. According to the Roman Catholic and Orthodox view, the practice of the eighth century in this respect was

[1] *Protrept.*, iv. 55

Holy Images

right and agreeable to the fundamental principles of Christianity: according to Protestants, it was a lapse from the original Christianity into pagan superstition. Catholic and Orthodox scholars are thus disposed to carry back the use of pictures and images to the first generations of Christians; Protestant scholars to maintain that the Church of the first three centuries at any rate was, as a whole, staunch against any veneration of images and shy of images and pictures altogether. The controversy is one as to facts; it turns upon the valuation of our fragmentary evidence. The data are of two kinds, archaeological and literary—the remains, that is, of decorated objects made by early Christians and what survives of early Christian writings. And here we find that the two kinds of evidence seem to yield somewhat different results. The strength of the Catholic case is archaeological: it is on the basis of more extensive study of the remains of early Christian art that Carl Maria Kaufmann in his *Handbuch der Christlichen Archäologie* (Paderborn, second edition, 1913) can treat the supposed image-hating temper of early Christianity as a long-exploded myth: the strength of the Protestant case is in the words of early Christian writers and assemblies. There must, of course, be some way of reconciling the two kinds of *data*. Catholics, taking the remains of early Christian pictorial and plastic art to show the real mind of the Church, sometimes explain away what seems the literary evidence on the other side: utterances in condemnation of images do not really mean what they seem to mean, or they are utterances of heretical puritans like Tertullian, which cannot be taken as typical. Protestants, confronted with the archaeological evidence, say one or other of two things: (1) that the dating of the remains is very conjectural, and that

Early Christian Paintings

Catholic archaeologists probably make them earlier than they really are; (2) that they represent a popular practice in the Christian Church which did not accord with the better mind of the Church, as represented by its outstanding writers and higher authorities.

If the dating of frescoes in the burial-places, at Rome or elsewhere, arrived at to-day by some specialists in this branch of archaeology is correct, then members of the Christian community were having their tombs decorated with paintings as far back as the first century—at a time, that is, when there were still people alive who had seen the Lord and the latest books of the New Testament had not yet been written.[1] These earliest Christian paintings (done possibly by pagan craftsmen under Christian direction) show no shyness in the matter of representing the human form. Many of them relate to stories in the Bible, in which men and women, no less than animals, are freely depicted. Yet there is something in the selection of subjects in these earliest Christian paintings which seems to show a shyness not felt by later Christians. Representations of the Deity are, of course, avoided: God, acting from heaven, is symbolized only by a head or arm, where the scene is Abraham about to sacrifice Isaac or Moses receiving the Law, just as in the Jewish frescoes at Dura. In regard to Jesus, it is remarkable that the events of the Passion are avoided. There is no Christian representation of Christ upon the Cross till after Constantine. The oldest picture of the Crucifixion known is the caricature scrawled by some heathen mocker

---

[1] Against this, W. Elliger, *Zur Entstehung d. christ. Bildkunst*, pp. 22–8, argues in disproof of the evidence adduced from the monuments, which purports to show that the beginnings of Christian painting go back earlier than the middle of the second century.

Holy Images

on the walls of the Imperial Palace in Rome, in which the Crucified is given an ass's head and the figure of the Christian whom the mockery was intended to annoy was rudely sketched beside the cross with the words below: "Alexamenos worships God." What is stranger is that during the first three centuries of Christianity the Cross itself does not appear in use as a symbol. This is all the more strange in that from the literary evidence, from the Epistle of Barnabas and from Justin Martyr, we know that early in the second century mystical significance was attached by Christians to the shape of the Cross, whether it was thought of as in the T-shape, as by Barnabas, or in the shape familiar to us, as apparently by St. Justin. Yet it is never found visibly represented in the remains of early Christian art. It seems to have been Constantine himself who caused the Cross to come into general use as a Christian symbol. According to the well-known story, a phenomenon in the sky—possibly that which we call "mock suns"—had seemed to him to present the form of the Cross, and the Cross was accordingly embodied in the design of the new imperial banner, the labarum.[1]

[1] If it is hard for a historian to say what precise phenomenon gave rise to the account given by Eusebius, a contemporary, of the Cross in the sky said to have been seen by all Constantine's army in A.D. 312, a similar problem is offered by an alleged appearance no longer ago than December 17, 1826, at Migné in France. After a priest, preaching in the open air, had referred to the story of Constantine's Cross, a luminous cross about 80 feet long appeared in the air at about 100 feet, it would seem, from the ground, evident to all the assembled multitude of some three or four thousand people. It was five o'clock; the sun had set, and the sky was cloudless. We have the official account of this odd incident sent to the Prefect of the Department by the First Councillor of the Prefecture and the Report of a Commission which examined eye-witnesses of the event within a few weeks of its occurrence, and which included a Protestant who was a professor

[*By kind permission of the British Museum*

PLATE II.—CRUCIFIXION ON IVORY BOX IN THE BRITISH MUSEUM
(PAGE 99)

No Pictures of the Passion

When an ancient image of Apollo was given a new head to serve as a statue of Constantine on the top of the great column in Constantinople, the globe in the hand of the figure had a Cross set upon it. From the days of Constantine the use of the Cross as a symbol throughout the Christian world became common and forms of homage were soon addressed to it. The earliest known representations of the Crucifixion, in which the human figure of the Lord is shown upon the Cross, belong, so far as I can gather, to a date round about A.D. 400—a wooden door from Santa Sabina in Rome and a carved ivory box in the British Museum (see plate ii). In sixth-century-France the painting of Christ on the Cross in a church still excited such scandal that the bishop had to have it covered with a veil.[1]

But while representations of the suffering Christ were avoided in the Christian art of the first three centuries, there are paintings in the catacombs, put by some archaeologists early in the second century, which represent miracles of the Gospel story—the healing of the woman with an issue of blood, the healing of the paralytic man, the raising of Lazarus. There is also an equally early picture of the Baptism of Jesus. But in regard to these representations of Jesus, it is to be noted that the human figure drawn is believed by archaeologists to be intended rather as a symbol, than as a portrait, of the

---

of physical science. The story is told with further details by Father Herbert Thurston, S.J., in his little book *Beauraing* (Burns Oates & Washbourne, 1934). We need not wonder that it is sometimes difficult to determine what facts lie behind the documents of one thousand six hundred years ago, when a plausible explanation for an event so near our own time, in view of all the *data*, does not readily offer.

[1] Gregory of Tours, *De Gloria Martyrum*, ch. 20.

Holy Images

Person. The type is beardless, and often has the appearance of a boy or lad—a figure such as might be derived from the tradition of an artistic school for the conventional representation of a young man. It is not till the third century that we begin to find pictures of a bearded Christ, in which the artist may be trying to show what he thinks that Jesus, as a man upon earth, really looked like. The symbolical character is quite clear in the figure of the Good Shepherd, which was so favourite a one with the early Christian artists. This appears already in tomb paintings ascribed by some to the first century. The type was the adaptation by Christian artists of a pagan one— Orpheus amongst the animals or Hermes *kriophoros* carrying a ram upon his shoulders. Sometimes Orpheus himself is represented with Phrygian cap, playing a lyre, in Christian catacombs, perhaps a parable of the Christ whose word draws lower creatures to Himself. In the Good Shepherd type the figure is always youthful, in short tunic, carrying a lamb or sheep upon His shoulders. The finest embodiment of the type is the statue in the Lateran, the work of some sculptor who was not meanly trained in the old Greek artistic tradition, commonly ascribed to a date round about 200 (see plate iii). Obviously this type is no more intended to be a portrait of Jesus than the figure of an old man to-day, in a picture illustrating the parable of the Prodigal Son, would be intended to be a portrait of God the Father. It was simply a conventional presentation of the type "Shepherd," according to the current artistic tradition, which for Christians would be a parable of the Good Shepherd, whom they trusted to carry them through the darkness of death to the abode of bliss beyond.

In addition to these representations of Jesus in His

[Alinari]

PLATE III.—STATUE OF THE GOOD SHEPHERD IN THE LATERAN (PAGE 100)

The Shepherd and the Child

different activities, there are quite early pictures of the infancy. The earliest in which the Mother is shown with the Holy Child upon her lap is said to be a fresco in the catacomb of Santa Priscilla; in the second century there are two pictures known, apparently representing the Annunciation, in which the Virgin is seen sitting, while the angel stands before her. But although all these pictures and carvings show that some Christians in very early Christian times were willing to have a human figure painted or carved representing the Lord or His Mother, a certain shyness is shown not only in the avoidances we have noted. That shyness may also be detected in the predominance of pictures illustrating Old Testament stories over pictures of the story of Jesus. Pictures of Noah in the ark (the ark being curiously represented as an open box, out of which Noah emerges like a surpliced clergyman in a pulpit), of Abraham's sacrifice, of Moses bringing water out of the rock, of the Three Children in the fiery furnace, of Daniel in the lions' den, are commoner than pictures relating to the Christian Gospel. No doubt, the Christians found consolation in the Old Testament stories, understood as parables. Still, the predominance of Old Testament subjects is remarkable. Some archaeologists would account for it as due to the *disciplina arcani*, according to which the mysteries of the faith might not be exhibited before the eyes of outsiders, and they would explain the relative increase of New Testament subjects after Constantine by the fact that now, in the Christian Empire, this prohibition was withdrawn. It may also be partly accounted for on the supposition that the Christians found a tradition already prevailing amongst the artists employed by members of the Jewish community, as we

Holy Images

saw that Dr. Kraeling suggests in connexion with the Jewish frescoes at Dura, and that conventional representations of the different Old Testament stories had already established themselves, so that a Christian, in giving orders for the decoration of a tomb, might find it simpler to tell the artist to execute the designs with which he was familiar. But perhaps neither of these two suppositions account completely for the backwardness of the Christian community to make pictorial representations of those events which for them were the holiest events in the history of mankind. It is difficult not to think that we may here see a feeling that by giving material visibility to an idea regarded as peculiarly holy you have inevitably degraded or profaned it. It would not have been simply a submission to those precepts of the Mosaic Law which forbade the making of a similitude, if that was understood, as we have seen that it was by Jews in the first century, to forbid the making of the image of any living thing, or of human beings. That prohibition the Christian paintings and carvings anyway transgressed. It must have been some feeling that in itself the visible representation of the holy was wrong.

We may believe with more confidence in the existence of such a feeling amongst the early Christians because a similar feeling seems to have prevailed amongst the early Buddhists. A. Foucher has pointed out in his book, *The Beginnings of Buddhist Art* (pp. 4, 5), that in the earliest Buddhist bas-reliefs which we have, belonging to the second and the last century B.C., bas-reliefs which illustrate the life of the Buddha, there was evidently a feeling which forbade a representation of the Buddha himself except symbolically. In the various scenes in which the Buddha acts, while the other persons are shown in

[*By kind permission of the British Museum*

PLATE IV.—SCENE FROM THE LIFE OF THE BUDDHA IN THE AMRAVATI SCULPTURES

(PAGE 103)

Scenes in the Life of the Buddha

bodily form, the presence of the Buddha is indicated only by symbols such as two footprints or an empty throne (see plate iv). About the time of the Christian era the artistic school of the Gandhara country, on the North-West frontier, became prominent. This school was under predominant Greek influence—whether from the Greek or semi-Greek dynasties which had held sway in that part of the world since Alexander the Great or from commercial intercourse with the Roman Empire. Greek artists had no compunction about making images of gods, and it seems to have been Greek artists who first invented for Buddhists, some 500 years after the death of the Buddha, a type representing their Founder. In Buddhist sculptures subsequent to the Gandhara school, the Buddha himself is freely portrayed where scenes of his story are represented. The type familiar to us of the Buddha sitting cross-legged, as common to-day in Buddhist countries from Ceylon to Japan as the crucifix is in Roman Catholic Europe, has become Orientalized to an extent which obliterates the traces of its Greek origin. But the remains of the Gandhara sculpture seem to give us intermediate stages between the type as it first took shape in the mind of an artist trained in the Greek tradition and the type as it became general in India and the further East.

Looking then at the archaeological remains of primitive Christianity we should say that, while there is a total absence of paintings or images as things to which any form of homage is directed, and while there seems to be a feeling of shyness in representing the holiest elements in the Christian story, while also the Person of the Lord is not shown for at least two centuries except by figures understood as symbolical, there is an apparent freedom,

Holy Images

from the second century onwards, in regard to pictures or sculptures representing human beings. The Second Commandment, as understood by Jews of strict observance, does not seem to be regarded as binding. When we turn to the literary evidence, we get, as was said, a different impression.

In the Christian writings of the first three centuries we do not, of course, find any explicit statement that it is wrong for Christians to make pictures or images of anything or of the persons whom they regard with religious reverence, or of the Lord Jesus in particular. They never take note of the fact that Christians are, as a matter of fact, decorating their tombs with pictures of the kind we have just seen, and condemn the practice as evil. The idea that Christians could make representations of Christ, of His Mother, and of the apostles, seems never to occur to them, unless one includes amongst Christians the heretical Carpocratians of whom Irenaeus wrote in an often-quoted passage:

"They call themselves Gnostics and have certain representations, some in painting, some fashioned in other material, asserting them to reproduce the portrait of Christ made by Pilate at the time when Jesus was here with men. These images they decorate with wreaths and display them side by side with the statues of the philosophers of this world, to wit, Pythagoras, Plato, Aristotle and the rest, and they use all the other observances in regard to them which pagans are wont to do." (i. 25. 6.)

From this passage Protestant scholars commonly infer that Irenaeus considered it wrong for Christians to make visible representations of the Lord: the Roman Catholic A. Knoepfler, on the other hand, contends that what Irenaeus found offensive was not the fact in itself that

Literary Evidence

the Carpocratians had images of Christ, but their claim that these images reproduced a portrait made by Pilate and their addressing the same forms of reverence to the images of pagan philosophers as they do to those of Christ.[1] This is hardly the natural meaning of the passage in its context: but the passage cannot be considered conclusive proof that Irenaeus thought all representations of Christ wrong.

Tertullian indeed once refers to representations of the Good Shepherd upon cups used by Christians. He does not distinctly call it wrong, but it comes in a context of rhetorical mockery. Tertullian had a particular hatred of the writing by Hermas, entitled *The Shepherd*, because it allowed the re-admission of fornicators, if penitent, to communion. The figure of the Shepherd was thus associated in his mind with the plea for moral laxity in the Church. He describes it in his rhetorical way as the "idol of drunkenness and sanctuary of adultery," and the Christians who, at the Eucharist, drank out of a chalice with the figure of the Good Shepherd engraved upon it, while counting on the liberty to sin afforded by the possibility of a second repentance, had, he declares with bitter irony, chosen their symbol well.[2] This passage, again, yields no clear statement about the making of images in general. Tertullian certainly treats this particular symbol with contempt, but he might be treating it with contempt only as used by the Christians whom he thinks so unworthy.

---

[1] *Der angebliche Kunsthass der ersten Christen* (included in the *Festschrift Georg von Hertling zum 70ten Geburtstag dargebracht*: Kempten and Munich, 1913). I know this essay only through the quotations from it in Hugo Koch, *Die altchristliche Bilderfrage* (*Forschungen zur Religion u. Liter. der Alt. und Neu. Testaments*, Göttingen, 1917).

[2] *De Pudicitia*, 10.

Holy Images

What any of these writers would have said on the general question, had it been put to them, we can infer only from the principles which seem implied in their utterances regarding pagan idolatry. Some of these utterances, as we have seen, imply that all making of pictures and images is wrong. This is plainest perhaps in Tertullian. In his work *De Idolatria*, he does in one passage contemplate someone raising an objection to the statement that God had forbidden the making of an image by adducing the brazen serpent. It is difficult to think that a pagan would have appealed to this incident in the Old Testament. Who could it be except a Christian who wanted to find a justification for the making of pictures and images in the Christian Church? Tertullian meets the objection by declaring that in this case God gave an exceptional command in order to pre-figure the Cross of Christ.[1] That did not invalidate His general Law, the Second Commandment. "If in both cases you acknowledge one and the same God, there you have His Law, 'Thou shalt make no likeness.' If you take account of His command to make a similitude later on, well, do you imitate Moses: before you make any similitude contrary to the Law, wait till God has given you the order." It is

[1] The difficulty of the brazen serpent had already been raised by Justin (*Dial. c. Tryph.*, 112) and explained in the same way as by Tertullian. It also constituted a problem for the Rabbis later on, though, since the representation of all living creatures belonging to the earth, except men and dragons, was, as we have seen, generally regarded by the Rabbis as permissible, there was no conflict apparent between Moses making the brazen serpent and the Second Commandment. From the passages about the brazen serpent in Rabbinical Literature which Professor Loewe has very kindly looked up for me I gather that the problem for the Rabbis was not so much "Why an image?" as "Why the image of a *saraph* (a fiery serpent, a seraph)?" and "Why of brass?"

Tertullian and the Alexandrines

taken for granted here—that is important to notice—that the Second Commandment is still binding upon Christians. Again, those utterances of Tertullian, already alluded to, in which he condemns the making of pictures or images on the ground that they are untrue, a fallacious appearance, a lie, would apply as much to images made by Christians of the objects of their devotion as it would to the images made by pagans. Tertullian, however, as someone whose puritan views conflicted with those of the Catholic Church generally, may well be surrendered by those who defend the use of images in the Christian Church to the other side without their case being thereby weakened.

The arguments used by the Alexandrine Fathers, Clement and Origen, against pagan idolatry would apply to any making of images, or at any rate to any making of images for worship—the idea especially that to have a visible object before you in worship did not help you to reach the unseen Reality beyond or behind, but was a snare which hindered the mind from rising. Clement cites with approval the precept attributed to Pythagoras: "Ye shall not wear signet rings whereon are engraved representations of the gods" and adds: "Similarly Moses made an express and public Law against the making of any carved or molten or moulded or painted image and representation, in order that we might not direct our attention to sensible objects, $αἰσθητά$, but might proceed to the intelligential, $τὰ\ νοητά$."[1] And Origen, as we have seen, condemns pagan image-worship on the ground that a visible symbol drags the soul down to earth from God. When early Christian writers want to contrast, with the pagan's direction of his worship to the

[1] *Stromata*, v. 5, 28, 4.

Holy Images

image of a god, the true mode of worship, it is never the direction of worship to a Christian manufactured symbol which is shown as the antithesis; it is the elevation of mind to the invisible Reality direct. The only image of God to which reverence of a kind should be paid is the image made by God Himself in man: "It is we, we who carry about the similitude of God in this living, moving image, Man, an image which always dwells with us, counsels us, bears us company."[1]

It has, of course, to be recognized that language may be used depreciative of the use of images in worship as compared with the direct apprehension of the invisible, without it being necessarily implied that all use of images is wrong or forbidden to worshippers on the lower plane. We may see this by Porphyry's letter to his wife Marcella. "The teaching tells us that the Deity is present everywhere and in all circumstances. The temple which has been dedicated to Him by man is, in a special sense, the mind of the wise man—that alone. . . . It is the office of the wise man to adorn for God by wisdom a sanctuary in his thoughts, having for image therein, to glorify God withal, his *nous*, the living image of God, which God has fashioned within Him. . . ."[2] "The sacrifices of the unwise are but fuel for the fire, and the dedications of the unwise do but provide temple-robbers with the means to gratify their lusts. For you must let the temple of God be the spirit within you, that temple you must prepare and adorn to make it fit to receive God."[3]

If we had such language by itself, we might easily suppose that the writer was someone opposed to all pagan image-worship. But Porphyry was the principal champion of Greek paganism against Christianity. In the

[1] *Protrept.*, iv. 59, 2.   [2] *Ad Marcellam*, § 11.   [3] § 19.

Porphyry and Asterius

same letter to his wife he indicates that he regards it as an impiety if anyone neglects the images of the gods, although a less heinous impiety than if someone attaches to the gods the unworthy conceptions which the vulgar do.[1] This depreciation of a worship which uses material images is relative only. The parallel should teach us to be cautious, in the case of Christian writers, how we take the language expressing a relative depreciation of visible symbols in worship to mean an absolute repudiation of visible symbols. For instance, a writer round about A.D. 400, Asterius, Bishop of Amasea, in a sermon refers to the fashion of the day for Christians to have representations of Gospel scenes, Christ with His disciples, the raising of Lazarus and so on, woven upon their robes. "If they will take my advice," the bishop says, "they will sell such garments and pay honour to the living images of God. Do not paint a picture of Christ! That one humiliation of Him, when He took upon Him humanity for our sakes of His own will, is enough. Rather carry about within your soul in spiritual wise the immaterial Logos. Do not have the paralytic man of the Gospel upon your clothes, but go to visit those who are bedridden. Do not look so steadfastly upon the sinful woman at the feet of the Lord, but have contrition for your own sins and shed tears yourself for *them*"—and so on. Yet the same bishop who writes this gives us in another work an emotional description of a picture which he had seen in a church representing the martyrdom of St. Euphemia, and he speaks of it as an established Christian custom to offer forms of homage to the symbol of the Cross.[2]

[1] Ch. 17.
[2] The passages from Asterius are given in translation in H. Koch, *Die altchristliche Bilderfrage*, pp. 65–8.

Holy Images

We seem to have in Eusebius, at the beginning of the fourth century, someone who definitely did consider it wrong for Christians to make representations of Christ other than such symbolical ones as the Good Shepherd type. When the sister of the Emperor Constantine, Constantia, wrote to him with the request that he would send her a picture of Christ, he replied rebuking the desire. To represent Christ in His Divine nature, he said, would be obviously impossible, but even His human nature was so steeped in Divine radiance that it could not be represented in inanimate colours and strokes of the brush. His disciples had not been able to look upon Him on the Mount of Transfiguration. How much more impossible would it be to represent His human nature as it is now in Heaven! Pagans, when they wanted to represent a god, could not do otherwise than depict a human form. But for Christians that was not fitting. If Constantia urged that she wanted only a picture of Christ as He was in His earthly humiliation, she should remember the Second Commandment, which forbids the making of anything on the earth as well as of anything in heaven. She can never, Eusebius says, have seen such a picture as she asks for in any church. All over the world such things were excluded from churches, and it was a matter of common knowledge that nothing of such a kind was permitted for Christians. Once he had come across a woman who possessed a picture of two male figures—he presumed two ancient philosophers—which she imagined to be portraits of Christ and of St. Paul. He took the picture away from her to obviate anything scandalous. He had even avoided showing the picture to anyone else, lest it should be supposed that Christians had portable representations of the objects of their

Eusebius on Pictures of Christ

worship, as the pagan idolaters had of theirs. Paul taught us to cling no longer to Christ after the flesh. There was a story about Simon Magus that certain impious heretics rendered homage to his picture painted in inanimate matter. He himself had seen a picture of Mani treated with observance by Manichaeans. All such modes of worship were forbidden to Christians. They acknowledged their Lord and Redeemer by preparing themselves to behold Him as God and zealously cleansing their hearts that they might have pure eyes wherewith to see Him. But if anyone could not wait for that vision face to face, and craved representations of the Redeemer now, the best portrait-painter was the word of God.[1]

This is an exceedingly important testimony to the view of the Christian Church generally at the beginning of the fourth century. Eusebius could not have appealed to the exclusion of pictures of Christ from churches generally, as a well-known fact, if the thing alleged had not been true. It is thus of no avail to discredit his opinion, as some Catholic writers have tried to do, on the ground that Eusebius was tainted with Arianism; for it is his testimony to the general view of the Church rather than the personal opinion of Eusebius which is important. And, as a matter of fact, there is nothing particularly Arian in the grounds upon which he condemns representations of Christ. On the contrary he condemns them by insisting upon His divinity.

Utterances of Eusebius in other writings have been brought forward as inconsistent with his condemnation

---

[1] The letter of Eusebius to Constantia has been reconstructed from various extracts given in different ecclesiastical documents. It is given in Migne (*Pat. Graec.*, 2, pp. 1545–9). For further references, see H. Koch, *Die altchristliche Bilderfrage*, p. 43.

Holy Images

of pictures of Christ in this letter to the Emperor's sister. He speaks apparently with approval of the sculptured representations of Daniel and of the Good Shepherd put up by Constantine on a fountain in Constantinople.[1] Unless his adulation of Constantine here gets the better of his true belief, we can only suppose that he thought the Good Shepherd type inoffensive because it did not claim to be a portrait. There is nothing, of course, in any of these utterances to indicate that Eusebius thought it wrong to make the statue of a man who was not an object of worship, that he took a view like the Jewish or Mohammedan one—or that apparently of Tertullian—that it was wrong to make any image of a man. He speaks with seeming approval of the statues of Constantine. His story of the supposed image of Christ put up at Panion in Northern Palestine by the woman whom He had healed of the issue of blood (so often adduced in the later Iconoclastic controversies)[2] does not really come into consideration, since Eusebius definitely states that the woman's showing her gratitude in this way was a following of heathen custom. The image in question was almost certainly not an image of Christ at all, but an old pagan image—it has been suggested of Asklepios—near the sanctuary of Pan at the source of the Jordan, which in the time of Eusebius had come by popular Christian legend to be connected with the woman of the Gospel story.

[1] *Vita Const.*, iii. 49. [2] *Hist. Ecc.*, vii. 18.

LECTURE IV

We have seen that up to the time of Constantine, during the first three centuries of the Christian Church, the chief Christian writers show either a disapproval of any making of images—Tertullian and Clement of Alexandria—or at any rate a disapproval of images of Christ, while the archaeological evidence proves that, if a large number of Christians did not object to their sepulchres being decorated with Biblical scenes, they did at any rate shrink from making portraits of Christ or depicting the events of the Passion. There is no allusion, I believe, in Christian literature to a crucifix—a detached cross with the human figure upon it—before the seventh century. But beside the utterances of Christian writers and the remains of early Christian art we have to consider the early Christian regulations promulgated by assemblies or put together in books of Church Order. In our last lectures we glanced at pronouncements in two of these collections which seemed to make the very handicraft of a painter or sculptor incompatible with Church membership, but we saw that such pronouncements might be understood as referring only to the makers of pagan pictures and images. It has also to be recognized that the regulations contained in these documents may reflect the ideas of a local church or a particular group, not those of the Church as a whole.

There is, however, one pronouncement which expressly refers to Christian paintings and takes a prominent place in all discussions of the use of imagery by

Holy Images

Christians, a pronouncement which belongs to the threshold of the period in which the use of images became without controversy extensive in the Christian Church —the 36th Canon of the Synod which met at Elvira in Spain in one of the early years of the fourth century,[1] just before, or just after, Constantine, the new Emperor, had declared himself favourable to Christianity. *"Picturas in ecclesia esse non debere, ne quod colitur et adoratur in parietibus dipingatur"*—"There ought to be no pictures in a church (or in the Christian Church), lest the holy thing should be depicted on walls."

Round that sentence there has grown up a voluminous controversial literature. The Canon, it is claimed, does not forbid pictorial representations in catacombs underground, but forbids them in churches only, where the heathen might see them and be led to scrawl up caricatures of things sacred to Christians on the street walls; or the Canon forbids a particular kind of bad Church art which had come into vogue in Spain about 300. Such expedients recent writers of the Roman communion have themselves renounced as futile. The ecclesiastical historian, F. X. Funk, in a work published in 1897, showed them to be untenable: he recognized that the Canon does forbid altogether the pictorial representation of the objects of Christian religious regard.[2] J. Tixeront, in his *Histoire des Dogmes* (seventh edition, 1928), rallies to the same view. It is possible, indeed, for Roman Catholics to admit frankly that this is correct, and at the same time deny that the Canons of the Synod

---

[1] Hefele put the date as 306: H. Leclercq, in his notes to the French translation of Hefele, holds that it was earlier, about 300.

[2] *Kirchengeschichtliche Abhandlungen und Untersuchungen*, vol. i, pp. 346–52.

The Synod of Elvira

of Elvira give the general mind of the Church. The prohibition of pictures, Tixeront says, applied to Spain only, and the Synod's view of the matter was soon repudiated by the Church as a whole. There is, however, no evidence that anywhere amongst Catholic Christians pictures of Christ had been sanctioned in churches before this period. The Canon proves indeed that some Christians in Spain had begun to decorate churches with sacred pictures: otherwise there would have been no occasion for the Synod's concerning itself with the question. It also proves that at this date the authorities of the Church in Spain deliberately set themselves against the practice.

But while some Catholic writers have wrested the language of the Canon in order to make it compatible with the present Roman view of the use of imagery in worship, it has also been misconstrued on the Protestant side as a declaration against the offering of homage to pictures. Harnack, amongst others, tried to read this into it.[1] This is unquestionably a mistake. The Canon does not say: "There are to be no pictures in church in order that what is painted on the walls may not be worshipped": it says: "There are to be no pictures in church in order that what is worshipped may not be painted on the walls." In this form, the two clauses might seem a tautology, as if they constituted a statement that something must not be done, in order that it may not be done. But the statement "that which is worshipped must not be painted on the walls" is not really equivalent in meaning to the statement: "Sacred pictures must not be painted in church." The emphasis is on the word "walls," and the explanatory clause derives its meaning from the current

---

[1] *The Expansion of Christianity in the First Three Centuries.* Second edition, vol. ii, p. 304.

Holy Images

idea that a picture was something derogatory to the divine because the substance upon which it was painted was material, and the colours used to paint it with were material stuff. It seemed essentially wrong that what was an object of religious worship should be painted on a *wall* which was mere wood or brick or stone, perishable matter. We shall find this idea later on given prominence, when the great attack upon images broke out in the eighth century. At the time of the Synod of Elvira the idea of offering homage to pictures and images had not, so far as we know, come up at all. It would never have occurred to the Synod to prohibit it. The question before the Synod was whether the Persons of the sacred story should be depicted at all in churches.

There are, of course, in regard to the use of pictures and images in worship, not two, but three, distinguishable views to consider. There is the view that all making of pictures and images, or at any rate all representation of persons religiously sacred, is wrong—the view of Jews and Moslems: there is secondly the view that pictures and images of sacred persons—with, it may be, some exceptions—are permissible in order to instruct simple minds in the sacred story, or make the story vivid to the imagination and so stimulate devotion, but that it is wrong to offer any forms of homage to pictures or images; and, thirdly, there is the view that it is right, not only to make pictures and images, but to address towards them signs of religious reverence—kissing, bowing, or prostration.

When the Roman Empire became Christian, the Church as a whole, as we have seen, held the second of these positions.

It hardly seems possible on our fragmentary documents

Epiphanius or Pseudo-Epiphanius

to trace, through these four and a quarter centuries, the process by which the Church moved from the second and first positions to the third. Only bits of evidence offer themselves here and there to show that things are moving in that direction. Strong opposition to pictures is evidence, of course, that the use of pictures is coming in, since no one feels strong antagonism to something which he does not feel to be a danger. At the beginning of the period we should have the most signal demonstration of this antagonism if the writings which were circulating among Iconoclasts in the eighth and ninth centuries as writings of Epiphanius, Bishop of Salamis in Cyprus from 367 to 403, were certainly genuine. A number of fragments from these writings have been preserved. In one of them we read how Epiphanius furiously tore a curtain he found in a village church in Palestine, because it had upon it a human figure—Christ or a saint. The other fragments denounce the pictorial representation of Christ, of saints and angels, as impious, with arguments resembling those used by Iconoclasts in the eighth and ninth centuries. But whether these writings, or any of them, were genuine, or whether they were fabrications of Iconoclastic propaganda is still a matter of controversy.[1] It seems probable that before

[1] The friends of images in the ninth century maintained that they were fabrications, and Catholic scholars have been disposed to take this view. The Protestant scholar Karl Holl, in a paper published in 1916, and included in his *Gesammelte Aufsätze zur Kirchengeschichte*, put forward an elaborate defence of them, as genuine Epiphanius. His arguments have been answered by the Orthodox scholar, Georg Ostrogorsky, who thinks he can prove the writings to be fabrications (*Studien zur Geschichte des byzant. Bilderstreites*, Breslau, 1929). The Protestant scholar, W. Elliger, pronounces that "*Ostrogorskys Versuch gegen Holl die Unechtheit der Schrift des Epiphanius gegen die Bilderverehrung zu erweisen ist nicht als gelungen anzusehen*" (*Entst. d. altchrist.*

Holy Images

the offering of homage to pictures and images the custom had come in of offering homage to the symbol of the Cross, which itself, as we saw in our last lecture, is not found on Christian monuments or objects of religious art before Constantine set the example in the labarum.

By the end of the fourth century it is plain that pictorial representations of religious subjects were common in the Christian Church and that the shyness in regard to them, which one detects in the first three centuries, had almost entirely disappeared. St. Basil (330–79), in a rhetorical homily on the martyrdom of Barlaam, calls on all proficient painters to depict the martyr's victorious conflict with suffering and he adds: "and let there be also represented in the picture the Master who ordained and judges the contest, Christ!" Basil's brother, Gregory of Nyssa, similarly describes a church in which another martyrdom with its grisly details was depicted, and in the middle of the picture was the figure of Christ in human form, described by Gregory also as the *agonothetes*, the Orderer of the contest. The contemporary of these two Cappadocian Fathers, the Syrian John Chrysostom (347–407), we are told, had a picture of St. Paul in front of him, when, wakeful at night, he studied St. Paul's epistles, and it is described how, when he looked up from the written text, the picture seemed to come to life and speak to him.[1] None of these utterances show yet an actual

Bildkunst, p. 106, note 4). Perhaps it is natural for a German Protestant to stand by Holl against a Russian Orthodox. Of course such a question is not capable of mathematical demonstration either way: the utmost either side can claim is a certain preponderance of probability, and in judging of probability, theological and national bias can hardly fail to come in. Personally it seems to me that Ostrogorsky has the best of the argument.

[1] From a fragment of a Life of St. John Chrysostom, quoted by St. John of Damascus (*De Imag. Oratio, I,* Migne xciv, 1277 C).

The Cappadocian Fathers and Augustine

transition from the second position in which pictures are valued as means of stimulus and instruction to the third position in which pictures are adored.

But Eastern Christianity had moved faster than Western Christianity in that direction. The younger contemporary of Chrysostom in the West, Augustine (354–430), still evidently felt religious paintings to be a danger. He does not, it is true, condemn them outright, except any attempt to represent God, apart from His incarnation in Jesus, in human form. To place in a Christian temple a picture in which God is shown sitting in Heaven with a visible right hand, is, from the Christian point of view, an impiety; whether any Christians had at that date actually attempted so to portray God, or whether Augustine is speaking only hypothetically of the way such a thing would be judged on Christian principles, if it occurred, does not seem clear.[1] In the Middle Ages representations of the Trinity in which God the Father appeared as an old man with a white beard became common; they would have been pronounced by Augustine to be blasphemous: Augustine's other references to Christian paintings are in a context which indicates depreciation. The reference indeed to pictures of Abraham sacrificing Isaac implies no judgment one way or the other: Augustine merely says that such pictures are so common that the Manichaean against whom he is writing can hardly have been ignorant of the story or forgotten

[1] "*Tale enim simulacrum Deo nefas est in Christiano templo collocare; multo magis in corde nefarium est, ubi vere est templum Dei.*"—*De Fide et Symbolo*, vii. (14). I feel little doubt myself that "*nefas est*" is here to be understood hypothetically, it *would* be an impiety, if such a thing were done. The present indicative is used to mean that Christian principles do now rule out such an action just as they rule out an anthropomorphic conception of God in the heart.

Holy Images

it.[1] But the reference to pictures of Christ and His disciples does indicate dislike: he is censuring people who suppose that Paul was a disciple of Jesus while Jesus was on earth, and he conjectures that they may have been misled by pictures painted on walls (*in parietibus*, the same word used for depreciation in the Canon of Elvira). "No wonder," Augustine adds, "if people who invent fictions are taken in by people who do painting" (if *fingentes* are deceived by *pingentes*).[2] The assonance seems intentionally chosen to comprise the two kinds of people in a common disparagement.

The other passage of Augustine has to do with the banquets which many members of the Christian Church now held at the tombs of the martyrs, as a mode of showing honour to the dead. Augustine denounces these as a very evil custom.[3] In this connexion he speaks of those who do homage to pictures and sepulchres. The tomb of a martyr must then often have exhibited a portrait of him and those who feasted at the tomb must have also performed homage to the picture. This is perhaps the first notice of the worship of pictures in the Christian Church. It was still evidently the practice of a section of Christians only, of the same section whose banquets seemed to Augustine a scandalous indulgence of the sensual appetite for food and wine. He does not, some Roman Catholic writers have urged, single out the adoration of pictures for condemnation: he condemns

---

[1] *Contra Faustum*, xxii. 73.

[2] *De Consensu Evangelistarum*, i. x. (16).

[3] Novi multos esse sepulcrorum et picturarum adoratores: novi multos esse qui luxuriosissime super mortuos bibant et, epulas cadaveribus exhibentes, super sepultos seipsos sepeliant, et voracitates ebrietatesque suas deputent religioni.—*De Moribus Ecclesiae Catholicae*, xxxiv. (75).

Augustine on Sepulchral Banquets

only the unseemly indulgence at these banquets. But when he calls the people concerned *sepulcrorum et picturarum adoratores*, the phrase certainly implies a relative depreciation of this mode of honouring the heroic dead.

No utterance of Augustine suggests that religious pictures might be a help to devotion, as the utterances just quoted from the Eastern Fathers of his time certainly do. But even if Augustine had recognized that pictorial art might be serviceable in that way, it is probable that he would still have thought it dangerous. Elliger in this connexion brings in for comparison Augustine's attitude to Church music, and this bears so directly upon the general problem of the use and the danger of appeals to the senses in religion—the problem which is more or less before us all through these lectures—that we may well spend a moment here in considering it. Augustine was by temperament as sensitive to the appeal of music as to the appeal of language—"the pleasures of the ears" he calls them. "Sometimes," he says in the *Confessions*, "I seem to myself to attribute to them a higher value than is right, when I feel how our souls are moved more religiously, more ardently, to a flame of devotion by the actual holy words, let them be sung in a particular manner, and how every emotion of our spirit has its proper mode in voice and song, according to the peculiar character of the sound by which that particular emotion is aroused in virtue of some hidden affinity. . . . When I think of all the tears called forth from me in the first days after my conversion by the hymns of the Church, when I consider that even now I am moved, though it is now less by the singing than by the things sung, when these things are sung in a lovely voice with appro-

Holy Images

priate modulation, I recognize the great use of music."[1] At the same time Augustine felt that the appeal to the senses, which might help to lift the soul, might also retain it and hold it back. Pleasure in music seemed to him sometimes a delight of the flesh which unstrung the mind. There were times when he was carried in the direction of puritanism to a length which he himself afterwards recognized to have been wrong: he could have wished at those times that all those delightful tunes wedded in Church practice to the ancient psalms might be removed altogether from his ears and from the ears of Christians generally, and that the psalms might be simply read in an ordinary speaking voice, as had been done in Alexandria under Athanasius. "Thus," he says, "I fluctuate to and fro between the peril of pleasure and the experience of wholesome help." On the whole he was disposed, though with hesitation and doubt, to approve of music in the Church, "in order that through a gratification of the ears the weaker souls may be lifted to feelings of devotion." "When, however, I catch myself being more moved by the singing than the things sung, I confess that I have fallen into punishable sin, and then I would wish all sound of music away."

This fear of aesthetic pleasure no doubt seems to us to-day mistaken and morbid. It would be well, perhaps, for Catholics like the late Mr. Chesterton, who are always lashing Protestant Puritanism, to remember that the Christians of the early Church went much further in Puritanism than the Puritans of the seventeenth and nineteenth centuries did. Even Scottish Presbyterians of the more rigorous generations had no dread of singing psalms. But if St. Augustine's fear of musical pleasure

[1] *Confess.*, x. 33, §§ 49, 50.

The Pleasures of Ears and Eyes

was excessive, there really is, unless the considerations we have had before us in these lectures mislead, in the case of all aesthetic appeals used in religion as a means to lead to something beyond themselves, a liability for the means to draw the interest to themselves, and so hinder the process they were meant to further. Augustine's fluctuation between thought of the possibility on one side and thought of the possibility on the other side was therefore not entirely absurd and vain. He had the sense of a danger that was really there. And the same principles by which he judged appeals to the musical ear had application to the appeal of visible imagery. Of this Augustine was himself conscious. If he was sensitive to music, he was sensitive also to visible beauty. Besides, here the element in his philosophy which he derived from Platonism came in. Visible beauty was an image or symbol of the Divine beauty which could be apprehended only by the mind. An apology for art might have been built upon this belief. "The beautiful things," Augustine writes, "transmitted through the souls of artists to their hands come from that Beauty which is above all souls, that Beauty for which my soul sighs day and night. Those who make external beauties or who follow after them draw indeed from that supreme Beauty their standards of appreciation, but they fail to draw from it their standards for the use of visible things. That supreme Beauty is there all the time and they see it not, so as to go no more far astray but keep their powers for Thee instead of squandering them in delights that end in weariness. I who say these things and perceive them distinctly, I too find my feet caught in these lower beauties."[1] In the end Augustine frames no apology for

[1] *Confess.*, x. 34, § 53.

Holy Images

art: the power of the visible beauties to retain for themselves the interest which ought to be directed to the supreme intelligential Beauty, to God, is far more present to his thought than their possible use as a means of apprehending the supreme Beauty. They are predominantly snares. If this was largely the case even with the pleasures of the ears, which did not involve the representation of a visible form, it must have been much more the case with pictures and images for Augustine, associated as such things were with the old pagan idolatry.

Another Christian writer contemporary with Augustine, Paulinus, Bishop of Nola (A.D. 353–431) names particular churches which were richly decorated with pictures of Biblical persons and scenes. Some of these paintings had been executed by the order of Paulinus himself. When he describes these as executed *raro more*, Hugo Koch has understood the phrase to mean that the pictorial decoration of churches was still something uncommon. The phrase may equally well mean that the Bishop took pride in the execution of these particular paintings as uncommonly good. Of the Biblical scenes depicted we know only that they were taken from the New Testament as well as from the Old. Christ in some of them was represented symbolically as a lamb. In a scene representing the Last Judgment the Lamb was shown standing on a rock with sheep on one side and goats on the other. What is more surprising is that amongst the pictures there is mentioned a representation of the Trinity in mosaic. The representation avoids human figures: the Father was symbolized by some emblem standing for a voice of thunder from heaven, perhaps the conventional representation of a thunderbolt,

Paulinus of Nola

the Son by a lamb, and the Spirit by a dove.[1] The correspondence of Paulinus also shows us pictures of people still living sometimes put up in churches. Sulpicius Severus, known himself as a writer, had begged Paulinus in a letter to send his own portrait to be placed in a church, as well as a portrait of another eminent contemporary Christian, St. Martin of Tours. Paulinus naturally uses in reply language which deprecates such an idea. Why should anyone want a picture of his outside earthly man? But he does not condemn the notion, as Eusebius had condemned the notion of a picture of Christ. Indeed, he sent the portrait asked for. He only stipulated that it should be regarded as the picture of a repentant sinner, not that of a saint like Martin.[2]

But there is still no idea in anything which Paulinus says of the addressing of homage to pictures or images. He justifies pictures simply as instructing the unlearned in the sacred story, or as attracting people to church from lower sensual pleasures or pagan religion. If we look on two hundred years we find Western Christendom still in its authoritative representative standing firm in the second position, upholding the use of pictures on the one hand, and condemning the worship of them on the other. The pronouncement of the great Pope, Gregory I (about A.D. 600), is classical in this connexion and has a prominent place in all discussions of images in the Christian Church. Bishop Serenus of Marseilles

---

[1] Pleno coruscat Trinitas mysterio:
Stat Christus agno, vox Patris caelo tonat,
Et per Columbam Spiritus Sanctus fluit.
Epist., xxxii. 10.

It is difficult to see how a *voice* could be represented in mosaic!
[2] *Epist.*, xxxii. 2, 3.

Holy Images

had found his flock offering homage to pictures in a church, and had broken up the pictures to prevent what he regarded as an evil practice. Upon this he received a letter from Rome. "It has come to our ears," the Pope wrote, "that, fired with inconsiderate zeal, you have broken up the pictures (or images) of the saints on the ground that they ought not to be worshipped. That you forbade them to be worshipped, we altogether approve: but that you broke them up we pronounce to have been wrong. It is one thing to offer homage to (*adorare*) a picture, and quite another thing to learn, by a story told in a picture, to what homage ought to be offered. For that which a written document is to those who can read that a picture is to the unlettered who look at it. Even the unlearned see in that what course they ought to follow, even those who do not know the alphabet can read there. Whence, for the heathen especially, a picture takes the place of a book. . . . If anyone desires to make images (i.e. here probably pictures), do not forbid him; only prohibit by all the means in your power the worshipping of images. I would have you, my brother, earnestly admonish your flock that from the sight of the story described they should conceive a more ardent sorrow for sin, and humbly prostrate themselves in homage to the almighty holy Trinity alone."[1]

---

[1] Perlatum siquidem ad nos fuerat quod inconsiderato zelo succensus sanctorum imagines, sub hac quasi excusatione ne adorari debuissent, confregeris. Et quidem, quia eas adorari vetuisses, omnino laudavimus; fregisse vero reprehendimus. . . . Aliud est enim picturam adorare, aliud per picturae historiam quid sit adorandum addiscere. Nam quod legentibus scriptura, hoc idiotis praestat pictura cernentibus, quia in ipsa etiam ignorantes vident quod sequi debeant, in ipsa legunt qui litteras nesciunt. Unde et praecipue gentibus pro lectione pictura

Pope Gregory I and Nilus

A classical utterance! In Eastern Christianity two centuries before Gregory the use of pictures in church had been defended on precisely the same grounds, in a writing of the monk Nilus, who is now believed to have belonged to the neighbourhood of Angora. He wrote a letter of censure to an imperial official who purposed decorating a church with hunting and fishing scenes and with a thousand crosses. Nilus describes such an idea as childish and foolish. One cross, he says, is enough, and instead of the hunting scenes it would be better to have stories from the Old and New Testament, painted by a really good artist "in order" (to translate his precise words) "that those who do not know letters and cannot read the Holy Scriptures may by gazing on the pictures have recalled to their minds the brave endurance of those who were sincere servants of the true God and be roused to emulation of their glorious and ever-to-be-praised exploits."[1]

Yet a century and a half after the letter of Pope Gregory to Bishop Serenus, the adoration of images and pictures has become common in the Christian world. The time at our disposal does not allow of our doing more than glance at the protest against image-worship

est. ... Frangi ergo non debuit quod non ad adorandum in ecclesiis, sed ad instruendas solummodo mentes fuit nescientium collocatum.

Si quis imagines facere voluerit, minime prohibe; adorari vero imagines modis omnibus veta. Sed hoc sollicite fraternitas tua admoneat, ut ex visione rei gestae ardorem compunctionis percipiant, et in adoratione solius omnipotentis sanctae Trinitatis humiliter prosternantur (*Epist.*, ix. 105, Migne 1027 f).

[1] ὅπως ἂν οἱ μὴ εἰδότες γράμματα μήτε δυνάμενοι τὰς θείας ἀναγινώσκειν γραφὰς τῇ θεωρίᾳ τῆς ζωγραφίας μνήμην λαμβάνωσιν τῆς τῶν γνησίως τῷ ἀληθινῷ Θεῷ δεδουλευκότων ἀνδραγαθίας, καὶ πρὸς ἅμιλλαν διεγείρωνται τῶν εὐκλεῶν καὶ ἀοιδίμων ἀριστευμάτων (*Epist. ad Olympiodorum Eparchum*, iv. 61).

Holy Images

embodied in the Iconoclastic movement, which was initiated by a public declaration of the Eastern Emperor Leo III against images in 726 and was not finally suppressed till after the death of the Emperor Theophilus in 842. It lies outside our present field to inquire how far the motives behind the movement were political, how far the struggle was a conflict between different elements in the State, or to trace the various events which marked the vicissitudes of the struggle.[1] It is rather the arguments brought forward on either side which concern us. Unfortunately we know little of those on the Iconoclastic side beyond what can be learnt from writings of the ultimately victorious friends of images. The principal defence of image-worship, put forward in the earlier phase of the struggle, was by a writer who looked on from a standpoint outside the Christian Empire, St. John of Damascus, who lived in Syria, a subject of the Moslem Caliph.

St. John approached the question of images as a philosopher whose ideas were in large part shaped by the Platonic tradition. No other Christian writer of those centuries, so far as the literature preserved goes, made so complete a survey of the arguments brought by the Iconoclasts and attempted to show with so little rhetorical vituperation that they were not valid. Some of St. John's reasonings bear only on the particular form which the problem of images had for Christians who accepted the Old Testament as inspired; some touch on fundamental

[1] There is of course a voluminous literature on the struggle between the Iconoclasts and the friends of images in the eighth and ninth century. References to earlier books and articles on the subject will be found in Dr. E. J. Martin's *History of the Iconoclastic Controversy* (S.P.C.K., 1930). I refer in this Lecture to one or two later contributions.

St. John of Damascus

principles which any consideration of appeals to the senses in religion should rightly take account of. His defence of image-worship is comprised in his three Orations Περὶ Εἰκόνων; but these three are not really wholly distinct works. There is a good deal of repetition between one and another, and Oration II may be regarded as a new edition of Oration I with modifications and additional matter. We may here consider St. John's arguments, not in the order in which these works give them, but according to the scheme of the general controversy. St. John's defence was to some extent based upon the defence of image-worship in a book against Judaism published by Leontius, a bishop of Neapolis in Cyprus, active in the latter part of the sixth century.[1]

One argument, put forward by St. John, and often afterwards by the friends of images, is an assertion in regard to historical fact which is plainly false—the assertion that the offering of homage to images was an original element in the tradition of the Church, that the Iconoclasts were innovators defying the authority of antiquity. It is simply absurd when St. John applies to the fairly recent custom of worshipping images the Old Testament prohibition: "Remove not the eternal landmarks, which thy fathers have set." (Prov. xxii. 28.) St. John and later controversialists in favour of image-worship ransacked the older Christian literature to find testimonies in favour of images: the result of their researches is given in various catenae of quotations, which were put forward both in circulated writings and in Church assemblies, notably in the second Council of Nicaea, the Council which finally made the rightness of image-worship a formulated dogma of the Church. None

[1] Migne, *Pat. Graec.*, xciv. col. 1565.

Holy Images

of the quotations from earlier writers, when looked at in their context, give any support to the case. Many of them refer to visual images in the imagination, or to man as the image of God, or something else quite different from a literal picture or an image of wood or stone made by man. The most celebrated of all these misapplications was the sentence from St. Basil, brought forward constantly in the eighth and ninth centuries and established afterwards in the tradition of the Roman Church as the classical statement of the principle by which image-worship is justified—ἡ τῆς εἰκόνος τιμὴ ἐπὶ τὸ πρωτότυπον διαβαίνει; in its Latin form, as still found in the Catechism of the Council of Trent, *honos qui imaginibus exhibetur refertur ad prototypa*, "the homage offered to images passes through them to the persons whom the images represent." St. Basil in that sentence was speaking of the Second Person of the Trinity, the Image of the Father, and what he asserted was that any honour offered to the Son passed through to the Father—his statement had nothing at all to do with material pictures and images. The misapplication was pointed out in the eighth century by the Iconoclasts, and the Patriarch Nicephorus on the other side in his Antirrheticus III[1] can only plead that Basil's statement about the Son involved a principle which applied also to material icons—which was to beg the question at issue.

All the voluminous attempts made by the friends of images to show that image-worship was an original part of the Christian tradition may therefore be set aside as futile, and the arguments put forward to justify the practice on its own merits may be considered. The controversy, it must be remembered, did not simply turn

[1] Migne, *Pat. Graec.*, vol. c. col. 404.

The Iconoclast Position

on the question whether homage should be offered to images and pictures, but also on the question whether images and pictures of Christ ought to be made at all. The Iconoclast position was not identical with that of modern Protestant communities, which do admit the use of pictures and images of Christ for instruction and adornment, although they condemn any worship of images: it was nearer to the position of Jews and Mohammedans and those early Christians who disapproved of any visible representations of sacred persons. So far as St. John of Damascus and the friends of images had simply to prove that the use of pictures was legitimate for the instruction of the unlearned and the kindling of devotion in the faithful, they were on the same ground as modern Reformed Christians, on the same ground as Pope Gregory I at the beginning of the seventh century.

Thus the arguments brought forward by St. John to prove the use of pictures as a means of instruction or of stimulus to devotion are likely to appear to most people to-day a proving of the obvious. The stock phrase "books of the unlearned" is used again by St. John. For those who cannot read the picture is a reminder. For those who do not know the Biblical story the picture may provoke question, like the twelve stones set up by Joshua in Jordan. "When your children shall ask their fathers in time to come, saying, What mean these stones? then shall ye let your children know, saying, Israel came over this Jordan on dry land." (Joshua iv. 21, 22.) The picture of Christ reminded Christians of their Saviour and called out a joy which the Devil envied them, and so he incited the Iconoclasts to have all pictures destroyed (ii. 6). If St. John had stopped here, there would be nothing to bring his views on images into conflict

Holy Images

with that of modern Protestants. He did not stop here: it was necessary for him to show that it was right to worship pictures and images, that pictures and images were vehicles of miraculous power. Before, however, we examine his arguments on this head, we must look at his way of dealing with what seemed to many Christians in those days, and has seemed to many Christians since, the great barrier to any worship of pictures and images, the Second Commandment. That Commandment certainly forbids the offering of any kind of religious homage to the likeness of anything in heaven or on earth or under the earth: as understood by the Jews it forbade even the making of any representation of the human figure. The transgression of that Commandment had the special name of idolatry. It was especially the sin of idolatry with which the Christian Church from the beginning—this was undeniable—had taxed the old pagan world. The Iconoclasts maintained that the present worship of pictures and images in the Christian Church was no less idolatry.

The answer of St. John of Damascus to this objection takes a double line. On the one hand it asserts that the prohibition of the Second Commandment is not absolute; exceptions were allowed even in Old Testament times; what it really means to forbid is the offering to any created thing of the particular kind of worship, *latria*, which may be offered to God alone, and Christians do keep the Commandment; on the other hand, St. John asserts that Christians are under no obligation to keep the Commandment; they do, as a matter of fact, what the Commandment forbids; but they need not be troubled by that, seeing that Christians are no longer under the Jewish Law.

What of the Second Commandment?

These two lines do not seem altogether consistent, though perhaps they might be made consistent by some expansion and explanation. It might be claimed that what St. John meant to assert was a double sense in the Commandment: it embodied an eternal principle, and in that sense Christians still keep it; but it embodied that principle in the prohibition of certain particular acts, and in that sense Christians are under no obligation to keep it.

We will consider first the prohibition in the Second Commandment, if understood as forbidding men even to make the image of any living thing. The prohibition was plainly not absolute. We have seen that Jews contemporary with St. John do not seem, as a matter of fact, to have put this construction upon the Commandment: no representation of the human figure might be made, but representations of animals (other than dragons) were not forbidden. Contemporary Mohammedans, however, did hold that it was against the Commandment of God for men to make the image or picture of any living thing. The Christian Iconoclasts, or some of them, may have understood the Commandment in the same sense: St. John was writing in a country under Moslem rule; it may therefore have seemed worth while to him to show that, in that sense, at any rate, the Commandment was sometimes not observed by persons in the Old Testament, even when acting under divine direction. Here you get the stock instances from the Old Testament brought up over and over again all through these controversies—the brazen serpent, the Cherubim over the ark in the Tabernacle, the Cherubim in Solomon's temple, the brazen oxen under the laver in Solomon's temple. The brazen oxen and probably even the brazen

Holy Images

serpent did not conflict with the Law, as contemporary Rabbis understood it; but the Cherubim most certainly did, since the image of any heavenly being was unlawful. But Jews in this case took the position that God could dispense with His own Laws and command in a particular case what was normally unlawful, and it was open to the Christian Iconoclasts to take the same view. They would not, therefore, have regarded these exceptional cases in the Old Testament as authorizing Christians generally to make images.

While, however, it might be questioned whether the Second Commandment forbade all making of images, or only the making of some particular kinds of images, St. John and the Catholic Church generally of his time agreed that it forbade the making of any image of God. That, the Christian friends of images continually assert, they recognize to be impious. This raised the problem of pictures or images of Christ; for Christ the Church affirmed to be God. St. John and the friends of images met this difficulty by emphasizing the distinction between the Divine Nature and the Human Nature of Christ. The Incarnation had made a great difference. It had been wrong for the Jews to make any image of God because (as Deuteronomy said) they had "seen no similitude." But now God had shown Himself on earth in visible form. Jesus was Man as well as God, and as Man He had a visible body which could be portrayed. It was, of course, only of His Human Nature, not of His Divine Nature, that a likeness could be made. At this point the question of images is brought on to the field of Christological controversies. It seems almost certain that the Monophysite way of regarding Christ influenced the Isaurian Emperors who opened war on the images in

Monophysite Influence

the eighth century, coming as Leo III did from a region of Asia Minor, where he may in his youth have been in contact with Monophysite Christians. The distinction which the Orthodox Church made between the Divine Nature and the Human Nature of Christ was precisely what the Monophysites abhorred. The Divine and Human were so fused in Christ that you could not consider either of them apart from the other. Thus a picture of Christ, according to the Monophysites, could not fail to be a picture of God, and a picture of God was impious because God was ἀπερίγραπτος, uncircumscribed, without an outline, and a picture necessarily drew an outline round the Figure presented. The Nestorians went further than the Orthodox Church in making a distinction between the two Natures, that Church holding a middle position between the Monophysite and the Nestorian extreme. The Iconoclasts thus naturally taxed the friends of images with being Nestorians, while the friends of images taxed the Iconoclasts with being Monophysites.

In St. John Damascene's defence of images the Christological question is very slightly touched on: it had not yet been put prominently forward in the controversy at that time: it was the charge of idolatry raised by the Iconoclasts that St. John had to meet. But the attack on images issued by Constantine V before the Iconoclast Council of 754 did lay stress on the Christological argument, and the charge of idolatry was dropped in the later phases of the controversy. The controversy came now to pivot on the question whether, apart from the question of worshipping a picture, any picture of Christ could lawfully be made. As God, the Iconoclasts contended, Christ was uncircumscribed. Yes, as God, the

Holy Images

Orthodox retorted; but not as Man: his human body was circumscribed, had an outline which a painter could draw.[1]

When St. John wrote, his main task was to show that images and pictures might not only be made, but might be worshipped, that such worship was not idolatry. What can St. John say on this head? His contention is here that the Second Commandment is not binding on Christians. It has been so generally taken for granted in Reformed Communions since the sixteenth century that the Decalogue declares the will of God for the conduct of Christians, that it has often seemed enough to point to the Second Commandment in order to convict the Roman Catholic and Orthodox Churches of idolatry. But St. John of Damascus looks at the Second Commandment without blenching. Quite so: that was a part of the Jewish Law, but Christians are not under the Jewish Law. A Protestant who argues against Catholic practice simply by adducing the Second Commandment is thus begging the question. It has first to be determined what part of the Mosaic Law remains of obligation for Christians, and what part does not. If, St. John says, you say that Christians must not offer homage to images, because it is forbidden in the Mosaic Law, you ought logically to abstain from eating pig and hare because it is forbidden in the Mosaic Law, and you

[1] A still more curious argument on the Iconoclast side was that a picture was ὁμοούσιος, of one substance, with its original. The *form* of the original found another embodiment in the image, but it was one and the same *form* in both. It was easy for the Orthodox to reply that this was true only of a living image, a son who had the same nature as his father, pre-eminently of the Divine Son who was consubstantial with the Father, but it was not true of a painted or sculptured image. We seem here in a tangle of scholastic subtleties.

The Problem of the Jewish Law

ought to have your son circumcised. There is nothing, it must be remembered, in the Old Testament to indicate that the Decalogue is throughout of more permanent obligation than the Mosaic dietary laws; the laws which Christians discard and the laws which they think still obligatory were not written with different letters in an ancient manuscript any more than they are printed in different type in our Bibles. When St. Paul declared that the Law was abrogated, and at the same time said that the righteousness of the Law was to continue to be exhibited in the conduct of Christians, he was really setting a problem before the Christian Church, the gravity of which we do not realize, because we are so accustomed to the demarcation which the Church eventually made between the still valid commandments, which we call moral, and the abrogated commandments, which we call ceremonial, that we suppose the line of division to have been much more obvious to the first generations of Gentile Christians than it really was. For the early Church not all the Ten Commandments fell under the division "moral": the commandment regarding the Sabbath was regarded as coming under the division "ceremonial"—as indeed seems appropriate to its character. When St. Augustine affirms that the Decalogue is still binding upon Christians, he excepts the Fourth Commandment regarding the Sabbath. No doubt, St. Augustine thought the Second Commandment still binding: but if you have once discarded any of the Ten Commandments as abrogated, you can no longer maintain the obligatoriness of any of the others simply because it is there amongst the Ten: you have to base the obligatoriness of each commandment on other special considerations, according to whatever you take to be the

Holy Images

principles determining right and wrong in conduct. If St. Augustine thought that one of the Ten Commandments was abrogated, it was open to St. John of Damascus to hold that two were abrogated, the Second as well as the Fourth.

The children of Israel were forbidden to make images or worship them, St. John maintained, because they were still in the childish condition, with a dangerous tendency to idolatry, idolatry being defined as the offering to a visible image that particular kind of adoration, *latria*, which should be rendered only to God. But Christians are no longer in the state of children and can be trusted to distinguish between the image of Christ and Christ Himself. The wise physician varies the treatment according to the condition and age of the patient: in the same way God forbade certain things to the ancient Israelites which are permissible for Christians.

When we think how the phrases of St. Paul, emphasizing the liberty of believers from external ordinances, were used at the Reformation for a discrediting of traditional Catholicism with its worship of images, it seems an irony of history when we read the same phrases used by St. John of Damascus for the defence of image-worship. Now it is those who would force upon Christians the prohibition of an old Jewish commandment who are turning back to the "weak and beggarly elements," who are denying the Gospel, who are renouncing the privilege of Christians to behold with unveiled face the glory of the Lord, in contrast with the old Israel, to whom it was not given to see God.

If you rule out any appeal to the Second Commandment as not relevant for Christian conduct, you have to consider the question whether it is right to offer homage

Christians Free from the Law

to pictures and images of Christ and the saints simply on the general principles of Christian religion. And here you find that the procedure followed, in order to justify all that extensive practice of image-worship in the eighth-century Church, which bore so strong an external resemblance to pagan idolatry, was a procedure followed in the justification of other questionable developments of Catholic religious practice. You seize upon certain modes of action, in regard to other things, universally recognized as natural and legitimate, and you insist that they involve a principle of which the whole vast practice objected to is only a logical extension. If you admit this common harmless practice, you must logically admit this other, and in this way a kind of ladder can be made from the common harmless practice, by which, before you can find any stopping-place, you have had logically to admit the lawfulness of the vast practice which in its total development had seemed to you so wrong. For consider. When you behold hundreds of Christians in churches prostrating themselves before pictures, murmuring prayers to pictures as if they were speaking to a living person, trying to derive supernatural benefits—healing, and so on—from material contact with the picture, putting trust in the presence of the picture to keep off various kinds of calamity, a wave of disgust may sweep over you: Christianity, you may feel, has sunk deep indeed in deplorable superstition. But here St. John would ask us whether we do not anyway perform many quasi-symbolical acts to show honour to particular persons, many acts which show a reverence for particular material objects. While it is true that there is a kind of worship which it is impious to offer to any but God alone, the Greek word we translate "worship,"

Holy Images

proskynēsis, literally a kissing of the ground in prostration, was actually used, St. John points out, in the Old Testament, of other kinds of reverential gestures legitimately addressed to things and men. (This, of course, is also true of the old English word "worship": it was quite commonly used of honour addressed to men —"with my body I thee worship" in the Anglican marriage service, "your worship" as a term of address to a magistrate, and so on.) St. John finds four kinds of worship, *proskynēsis*, mentioned without censure in the Old Testament, although the worship was not addressed to God. (1) Homage addressed to beings who can be described in a special sense as "friends of God," especially angels: when Joshua sees the angel by Jericho, the captain of the Lord's host, it is written that "he fell on his face to the earth and did worship" (Joshua v. 14). (2) Homage offered to holy places and things. "I will worship toward thy holy temple" (Psalm v. 7): "Worship the foot-stool of His feet" (so St. John read the text in his Septuagint) (Psalm xcix. 5). A text especially adduced in this connexion was one describing Jacob's last days in which our Bibles have only: "Israel bowed himself upon the bed's head," but the Septuagint has: "Israel worshipped towards the extremity of his staff." Since Jacob's staff was regarded as a type of the Cross, Catholics found in this text their warrant for acts of reverence directed to the Cross. (3) Homage addressed to other human persons set by the Divine order in a position of superior dignity and authority. In this sense, Jacob is said to worship his elder brother Esau, Joseph's brethren worship Joseph, Jacob worships Pharaoh; and, generally speaking, the homage offered to kings would come in here. (4) Worship may be addressed to equals, as a form

The Hallowing of Matter

of courtesy: Abraham is said to have worshipped the sons of Heth (Genesis xxiii. 12).

By such cases St. John seems to himself to have established satisfactorily by scriptural warrant the rightness of honorific bodily gestures—prostration and kissing—addressed to particular persons other than God and to particular material things. Why should one be so afraid of doing homage to a material thing made by the hands of men? In this fear St. John sees latent a view of matter, as essentially evil, which belongs to Manichaeism, not to Christianity. The worship addressed towards the Temple, spoken of in the quotation just given from the Psalms, was an instance of such homage. But there were numerous other things in the Old Testament which, if not exactly worshipped, were treated with especial reverence as holy—the Ark, the rod of Moses, the pot of manna kept in the Ark, and so on—all "base matter," all fashioned by the hands of men. And the Iconoclasts, against whom St. John was writing, did not hesitate to show reverence by bodily gestures to many material objects—the Cross, the Holy Sepulchre and other sacred places, the Holy Table, the ink and parchment of the written Gospels. Throughout, true religion recognized a hallowing of matter: Christ assumed a material Body. In all acts of religion, St. John insists, there is a bodily as well as a spiritual element—water *and* spirit in Baptism, the material voice-organs in prayer and psalmody, the matter of lights and of incense.[1]

A material object may acquire holiness by its associa-

[1] The idea that the representation of something holy by a picture was essentially derogatory because a picture consisted of material pigments upon a material wall, found already, as we saw, in the Canons of Elvira (pp. 115, 116), was current among Iconoclasts in the eighth century. Τὸν τοῖχον κονιάσαντες χρώμασι διηλλαγμένοις τὰς εἰκόνας

Holy Images

tion with a holy Person. The ground upon which Moses might not stand without removing his shoes had become holy by the presence of God in the bush. An image or picture is associated with its original by the visual likeness, in virtue of which it can serve to bring the Person portrayed to our mind, or make us realize him more vividly, and this association confers holiness on the material image or picture. That Christians did not regard the matter by itself as holy, St. John considers proved by the fact that when, by time or accident, a picture becomes defaced, no scruple is felt in burning the wooden board upon which the colours had been laid. Homage addressed to a picture is addressed really to the Person represented, Christ or Saint, and to him it passes through the picture, according to St. Basil's maxim.[1]

But behind all this argument there was something in the background which had an essential part in determining the attitude of the mass of Catholic Christians

ἀνετύπωσαν (Nicephorus adv. Epiph. frag). 1. Εἴ τις τὸν θεῖον τοῦ Θεοῦ Λόγου χαρακτῆρα κατὰ τὴν σάρκωσιν δι' ὑλικῶν χρωμάτων ἐπιτηδεύοι κατανοῆσαι καὶ μὴ ἐξ ὅλης καρδίας προσκυνῇ αὐτὸν ὄμμασιν νοεροῖς . . . ἀνάθεμα (Canon of the Iconoclastic Council of 754. Mansi. xiii. 336E).

[1] Compare the exposition of St. Theodore of Stadium in his letter to Plato. "The analogy of a mirror seems to me to fit. In the mirror there is, as it were, a picture of the beholder's face. But the likeness remains something detached from the matter of the mirror. If a man seemed to greet his own likeness in the mirror, he would not be embracing the matter of it. He did not approach the mirror for the sake of the matter, but of his likeness reproduced in the matter. It was for that reason he made contact with the matter. Of course, the moment he stands away from the mirror his similitude disappears too, showing that he had nothing in common with the matter of the mirror. So it is with the matter of the icon. When the likeness we saw in it, the ground of our act of homage, is effaced, the matter remains there, destitute of homage, having no longer any participation in the likeness" (Migne, xcix. p. 504).

Matter Charged With Power

in the eighth century towards pictures and images, and which St. John's *apologia*, so far as we have yet given it, has not taken account of. Icons were not thought of only as a means by which the Christian was reminded of Christ or of some Christian hero and through which he might express to Christ or to the Christian hero his feelings of reverence and gratitude. They were thought of—perhaps mainly—as things from which or through which supernatural power went forth to men. If St. John were to make an adequate defence of image-worship in the Christian Church, it was at this point that his task became critical. Yet for this too he found Old Testament precedents ready to hand—there was Elisha's staff, which if it did not actually succeed in recalling the dead boy to life when laid upon him, was certainly expected by the prophet to convey miraculous power. Another story tells how contact with the dead bones of Elisha did restore a dead man to life. But there were also cases mentioned in the New Testament in which material things, from their association with a holy person, conveyed supernatural power. The shadow of Peter, it is stated in Acts, was believed to heal sick persons upon whom it fell; the handkerchiefs and aprons brought from the body of St. Paul are stated in another passage of Acts to have really effected cures.[1] Anyone who accepted these passages as divinely inspired—and all Christians did—might perhaps question whether the association of a picture of St. Paul now painted with the person and will of the Apostle was as close as that of the handkerchiefs and aprons, was close enough to make it the vehicle of supernatural virtue, but he could not logically dispute St. John's general contention that a material thing might

[1] Acts xix. 12.

Holy Images

in certain cases from its association with the person of a saint, convey supernatural virtue. It is hardly possible to realize what words of immense reach in subsequent Christian practice St. Luke was writing when he penned that little sentence about the handkerchiefs and aprons carried from the body of St. Paul!

In choosing the terms to describe what it was about the sacred picture or image which made it the vehicle of supernatural power, it is interesting to observe that St. John, following no doubt the Orthodox tradition, used terms reminiscent of the story of the Annunciation in St. Luke's Gospel. Mary, as the recipient of an act of Divine Power which made her miraculously a mother, is called by the Angel κεχαριτωμένη, an object of especial *charis*, "Grace." "Thou has found *Grace* from God," the Angel also says. The regular phrase used of sacred icons is that the Grace and Power of God abides upon them. *Charis* seems to be thought of like some force, analogous to our ideas of electricity or magnetism or primitive man's idea of *mana*, residing in the picture or image. "The power of the Most High shall *overshadow* thee," the Angel says to Mary, and again this metaphor of "overshadowing" is regularly used to describe how the supernatural virtue passes into the icon.[1] This indicates that to the Christians of the eighth century the supreme example of the entrance of the Divine into the material sphere, the Word becoming Flesh, seemed to indicate the mode by which, in a lesser way, a Divine something might come to inform an image made by the

---

[1] The same word used by the Angel, ἐπισκιάζειν, is also used, as Norden has pointed out (*Geburt des Kindes*, 1924, p. 96), of the cloud which at the Transfiguration overshadows Jesus and the disciples, or, according to one reading, Jesus alone.

The Images Informed with Grace

hands of men. Much more might it inform those few images not wrought by the hands of men, in the existence of which Christians at that time believed—the *acheiropoieta*—such as the impression of Jesus's face upon a cloth which Jesus Himself, according to the legend, sent to Abgar, the prince of Edessa.

When once the belief was established amongst Christians that certain representations of Christ or of saints were charged with supernatural "grace" it was a short step to treat the images as if they were really persons. Theodore, the monk of Studium, the vehement champion of image-worship in the early part of the ninth century, in one of his letters congratulates a friend on having taken the image of a martyr to be sponsor at his child's christening. The martyr, he assures his friend, has been himself present at the ceremony and held in his own arm the child placed on the arm of the image. (This looks, by the way, as if the image in question had been a statue, not a picture.) "This," Theodore adds, "may seem incomprehensible, even incredible, to unholy ears and unbelieving hearts." The Emperor Michael II, "the Stammerer" (who was opposed to image-worship), in a letter written to the Western Emperor, Lewis the Pious, in A.D. 824, affirms that it was a common practice in Constantinople for images to be carried as sponsors to christenings, dressed up in linen clothes. Men taking monastic vows laid the hair they cut off in the lap of an image: priests scratched fragments of paint off the icons and mixed them with the elements in the Mass, or they placed the Host in the hands of an image, so that the communicant might receive it directly from the saint.[1]

[1] All allusions in modern books to these extravagant practices among Greek Christians in the ninth century are taken from this

Holy Images

For the Roman Church and the Orthodox Church of to-day the question of image-worship was decided in the sense of St. John of Damascus by the Second Council of Nicaea (787). Since the Council was attended by two Papal delegates and two Eastern monks who might be taken as representing the sees of Jerusalem, Antioch, and Alexandria, though they were never officially appointed, the Council is regarded by these two communions as Oecumenical, the Seventh General Council, and its decisions in consequence as infallible.

At this time Western Christianity had not yet as a whole gone as far as Eastern Christianity in the direction of image-worship. The Popes indeed no longer stood by the principle of their great predecessor, that it was right to have pictures in church, but wrong to worship them. Gregory III (himself an Oriental), Zacharias, Stephen II, Paul, Stephen III, Hadrian I, Paschal I—all of whom reigned between 731 and 827—committed themselves to an approval of image-worship. Yet perhaps even they did not go as far as the Eastern Christians did in personifying the images. At the Lateran Council of 769 held under Stephen III, while the rightness of venerating images was affirmed, it was felt necessary to append an explanation. "We do not venerate images as God, in the way the heathen do. We only (*tantummodo*) make the affection and charity of our soul correspond with the face painted in the picture." But that a great bulk of Western Christianity did not yet follow the Popes in their relative approval of image-worship was

letter of the Emperor Michael. It has to be remembered that the source is polemical. While there is no reason to doubt that the practices mentioned by the Emperor actually occurred, it may be that his picture is made blacker than the reality by his picking out precisely the worst cases of aberration.

The Caroline Books

made plain when Charlemagne in the last decade of the eighth century caused a definite manifesto against image-worship to be issued, which is preserved for us in the so-called Caroline Books. He expressly repudiated the decisions of the Second Council of Nicaea, and, in doing so, he had the support of a large number of the Western bishops; some modern experts believe that Alcuin the Englishman had a principal part in framing the manifesto. The attitude of Western Christianity is carefully distinguished from that of the Iconoclasts. It does not condemn the making of pictures and images and their exhibition in a church. It admits that images have their use for instructing the unlearned and stimulating devotion. Only it condemns the performing of acts of homage to them. Western Christianity is still in large part faithful to the ruling of St. Gregory—the *via media* between Iconoclasm and Image-worship.[1] The Council of Frankfort, attended by Churchmen from Gaul, Germany, Italy, Britain (794), seems to have endorsed the view of the Caroline Books on the question of images. In the reign of Charles's successor, Lewis the Pious, the second

---

[1] Roman Catholics commonly seek to mitigate the opposition between Charlemagne, with his Western bishops, and the Canons of the Second Council of Nicaea by urging that the Western bishops had before them only a Latin translation of the Canons which was exceedingly incorrect and in parts unintelligible. This is true, but defects of the translation do not account for the opposition; it is plain that the views of the Western bishops would have clashed with the Canons of the Council, had they had the Greek text before them, and understood it. It would be a mistake, however, to think that the doctrine of the Caroline Books agrees with that of the Protestant Reformers. They condemn image-worship indeed, but they strongly approve of the worship of relics. They argue that there is a real connexion between the person of the dead saint and a bit of his body or of his clothing, but no connexion at all between him and a fancy picture of him.

Holy Images

Emperor of the Holy Roman Empire, another ecclesiastical assembly took place in Paris (825). It strongly reaffirmed St. Gregory's *via media* and censured the late Pope Hadrian for the line he had taken. It drew up two letters to be sent by the Emperor to the present Pope Eugenius, one for forwarding to the Eastern Emperor, Michael. But after this our records fail us, and no adequate materials exist for tracing the process by which the West in the following time abandoned St. Gregory's ruling and went after Eastern Christianity in its cult of images. If the Reformed Churches are right in regarding this as superstition, it makes the tragedy more lamentable that it was a great Pope, a man belonging by his family to Rome, who had clearly and authoritatively laid down the true line in A.D. 600 and that Western Christendom was still sound two centuries later, when Greek Christendom as a whole had sunk deep in image-worship. In the course of time there came to be a difference between the practice in the two halves of Christendom. In the ninth century, as we saw, the icons worshipped in Constantinople were apparently statues as well as pictures; there has never been any formulated dogma in the Greek Church which condemns statues as wrong;[1] but general practice was governed by a feeling that images in the round were not seemly for Christians, only pictures in the flat, or very slightly raised. The test came to be whether you could or could not lay hold of the sacred figure's nose.[2] The West knew nothing of

[1] I am under obligations to Father F. Dvorník, the distinguished Czech authority on Orthodox Church History, and, through his means, to Prof. G. Ostrogorsky, for light on this point.

[2] Est illis hoc adagium receptum atque familiare: Nullam imaginem colendam esse, cujus nasum duobus possis digitis complecti (C. I. Ansaldi, O.P., *De sacro et publico apud ethnicos pictarum tabularum cultu* (second edition, Turin, 1768), p. 11).

Statues and Flat Icons

this distinction; their images in the round were as common as pictures. That the worship of a picture is less heinous than the worship of an image in the round can hardly be maintained, if we look at the matter from the point of view of the Reformed Churches. If the veneration of pictures is right, it was merely sound sense in the Western Church to sanction the veneration of statues as well. The idea that idolatrous aberrations might more easily follow from the use of images in the round than from that of pictures in the flat—an idea which, as we saw, is found in medieval Judaism—is obviously drawn from a naïve and untrue psychology. Its falseness becomes evident when we compare the cult of pictures in the Greek East with the veneration of images in the Catholic West. There has been in practice less superstition connected with the veneration of images in Western Catholicism than with sacred pictures in Greek and Russian Christianity.

We have seen that the controversy between the Pope and the bishops of Charlemagne in the ninth century, between the Roman Church and the Reformed Churches from the fifteenth century onward, has not turned on the question whether it is lawful to make pictures and images of Christ and the holy men of old—that is generally allowed to be unexceptionable—but on the question whether it is lawful to direct to such representations any forms of religious regard—bowing, kneeling, kissing, offering flowers and candles. On the principle that the homage offered externally to the image passes through it to the person represented, such forms of homage would be closely analogous to a man's taking off his hat when he passes the cenotaph in Parliament Street. He is not considered to commit an act of idolatry,

Holy Images

although he undeniably directs a gesture of reverence to a block of stone. On this principle the thinkers of the Western Church in the Middle Ages formulated a theory of the place of images in worship which clearly distinguishes the homage directed towards an image in Christian worship from idolatry. The homage, said Durandus (of St. Pourçain, died 1332), is not really directed to the image at all. It is directed to the person whom the image represents.[1]

The difference between this view and the view of the Greek Church comes out in the answer to the test question whether the homage offered to (or before) an image of Christ is *latria* or not. *Latria*, as has been already noted, is "worship" such as should be rendered to none but God, distinct from the kinds of veneration which it is proper to render to a very good human being or to any being inferior to God. If Jesus Christ is God the homage rendered to Him, according to Catholic belief, should be *latria*. On the principle then that the external gesture of homage directed to a picture of Christ or to a Cross is really directed to Christ Himself, through the medium of the picture or the Cross, it is an act of *latria*. This St. Thomas Aquinas affirms that it is: "As the Philosopher [Aristotle] says, the movement of soul towards the image is of a double character. It implies, for one thing, a movement towards the image, in so far as the image is a *thing* (a particular object) itself; it implies also a movement towards the image in so far as it is representative of a reality other than itself. Between these two movements there is this difference: the first kind of movement directed to the image as a particular thing, is *distinct* from the movement towards the reality repre-

[1] IV Sent. l. iii, qu. ix, a, 2.

St. Thomas Aquinas

sented, whereas the second movement, directed to the image as the representation of a reality not itself, is *identical* with the movement directed to the reality. Thus one must say that to an image of Christ, in so far as it is itself a particular thing (let us say, a carved bit of wood or a painted board), *no veneration at all* is offered, because veneration is owed to a rational being alone. It remains that veneration is exhibited towards the image, only in so far as it is an *image* (of something else); and thus it follows that the veneration exhibited to an image of Christ and the veneration exhibited to Christ Himself is one and the same. Since, therefore, Christ is adored with the worship of *latria*, it follows that the adoration directed to His image is an act of *latria*."[1]

All this is quite simple if one thinks of the acts of reverence we direct towards the cenotaph. There is a movement of my mind towards the cenotaph itself in so far as my senses show it to me as a stone object and I take notice of it. But when I take off my hat the movement of my mind is not to the cenotaph but to the multitude of dead men to whom I feel a special sense

[1] Respondeo dicendum quod, sicut Philosophus dicit, duplex est motus animae in imaginem: unus quidem in ipsam imaginem, secundum quod res quaedam est; alio modo in imaginem, in quantum est imago alterius; et inter hos duos motus est haec differentia, quia primus motus, quo quis movetur in imaginem, ut est res quaedam, est alius a motu qui est in rem; secundus autem motus, qui est in imaginem, in quantum est imago, est unus et idem cum illo qui est in rem. Sic ergo dicendum est quod imagini Christi, in quantum est res quaedam (puta lignum sculptum vel pictum), nulla reverentia exhibetur: quia reverentia non nisi rationali naturae debetur. Relinquitur ergo quod exhibeatur ei reverentia solum in quantum est imago; et sic sequitur quod eadem reverentia exhibeatur imagini Christi, et ipsi Christo. Cum ergo Christus adoretur adoratione latriae, consequens et quod eius imago sit adoratione latriae adoranda (*Summa*, Pars iii, *Quaest.* xxv, Art. 3).

Holy Images

of obligation. That desire to honour them is something distinct from my taking notice of the stone cenotaph; but the thought behind the gesture of reverence directed externally to the cenotaph is not distinct from the thought I direct to the dead; it is one and the same thought and feeling. Externally, indeed, my actions in regard to the cenotaph are not unlike some of the actions of a Catholic Christian in regard to an image. The gesture of uncovering the head and the gesture of bowing the head are pretty well equivalent, and just as the image may be garlanded with flowers, so wreaths of flowers are laid upon the cenotaph. But the homage is not addressed to the pillar of stone. Whatever character my feeling towards the dead may have, whether it is proper or improper, whether it is strong or weak, that is the character of my act of reverence. The stone cenotaph counts for no more than a means by which I declare my feeling towards the dead: my homage passes through the material symbol to the multitude of persons for whom the symbol stands —*refertur ad prototypa*.

Suppose, on the other hand, that in my acts of reverence directed externally to the cenotaph, there could be distinguished a homage to the dead and a homage of another inferior kind directed to the cenotaph itself, suppose that behind my action was a desire to honour the cenotaph distinguishable from my desire to honour the dead, I should, as St. Thomas indicates, be falsely endowing the stone object with a personality; homage can be offered to rational beings alone. If *latria* be the proper kind of worship to be addressed to Christ, then the whole of the homage I direct externally to a picture of Christ or a crucifix must be *latria*: if my act included an inferior kind of homage addressed to the image, dis-

Veneration Addressed to Images

tinguishable from the homage I address to Christ, then I am falsely making a person of the image. And to attribute personality to an image is the basic falsehood of idolatry.

This making of a distinction between the homage offered to the beings represented by the icons—Christ or His Mother or saints or angels—and the homage, of an inferior kind, offered to the icons themselves, is precisely what marked the doctrine of the Greek Church, as against the view formulated, as we have just seen, by St. Thomas. It was laid down most decisively that an honour was owed to the images themselves, an honour of the same kind for all images, whomsoever they might represent. For the persons represented indeed homage of very different modes was appropriate—the homage offered to Christ different from that offered to His Mother, the homage offered to His Mother different from that offered to an apostle, and so on. But the homage offered to an image of Christ was not different in kind from that offered to an image of the Virgin or of St. John: it was different only in degree. Thus the Greek Church did confer a kind of personality upon the icons, and feel that they had a claim to honour such as only a rational being can have.

An elaborate exposition of the question by V. Grumel from the point of view of a theologian who upholds Theodore of Studium against St. Thomas will be found in Vacant's *Dictionnaire de Théologie Catholique*, in the article "Culte des Images." The inferior kind of homage rendered to the images themselves is described in the *Terminus* ("Ορος) of the Second Council of Nicaea as τιμητικὴ προσκύνησις, "honorific homage" and distinguished from "real *latria*, which belongs only to the

Holy Images

Divine Being."[1] So too in the declaration of the Deacon Epiphanius.[2] Another way of distinguishing it is by the epithet σχετική "relative." The patriarch of Constantinople, who presided at the Council, Tarasius, is reported as saying: "and to these [the images] we offer homage with *relative* yearning, as to the name of Christ, who is God, and of our immaculate Lady the holy Mother of God ... while we offer our *latria* and our faith to the One True God alone."[3] So too in the (forged) letter which was circulated in the propaganda for the doctrine of the Second Council of Nicaea against the Iconoclasts, as having been written by Pope Gregory II to the Emperor Leo III, we read: "Men all over the world, when they beheld these things, left off performing acts of homage to the Devil and performed acts of homage to these images instead, not in the way of *latria* but of *relative* homage."[4]

What precisely "relative" means in this connexion may be a question. The answer would seem to be that whereas the homage offered to God or Christ or a saint is offered because of what God or Christ or the saint is in his own being, the homage offered to an image is not offered because of anything which that bit of matter is in itself, but only because of its likeness to the prototype, its *relation* to something other than itself.

---

[1] τὴν κατὰ πίστιν ἡμῶν ἀληθινὴν λατρείαν, ἣ πρέπει μόνῃ τῇ θείᾳ φύσει (Mansi xiii, col. 377).

[2] Mansi xiii, col. 309.

[3] Καὶ ταύτας σχετικῷ πόθῳ προσκυνοῦμεν, ὡς εἰς ὄνομα Χριστοῦ τοῦ Θεοῦ καὶ τῆς ἀχράντου δεσποίνης ἡμῶν τῆς ἁγίας Θεοτόκου ... πρόδηλον εἰς ἕνα μόνον Θεὸν ἀληθινὸν τὴν λατρείαν, καὶ τὴν πίστιν ἡμῶν ἀνατιθέμενοι (Mansi xii, col. 1086).

[4] οὐ λατρευτικῶς ἀλλὰ σχετικῶς (Mansi xii, col. 963).

Veneration according to the Orthodox

The thought of the Christian West in the Middle Ages, so long as it was exercised by itself upon the doctrine of the Church, could avoid the personification of wooden images into which Greek Christianity had fallen. St. Thomas had probably no exact knowledge of the controversy which had raged in the Greek Church in the eighth and ninth centuries or of the decisions of the Second Council of Nicaea, and was unaware of the disagreement between his doctrine and that of the Greeks. And if the Roman Church had followed its own way undeflected, the doctrine of St. Thomas would, we may conjecture, have become its approved doctrine on the question of images, as on so many other questions. The trouble was that by giving the Second Council of Nicaea the status of an Oecumenical Council whose decisions might not be questioned, the Roman Church could not in the end get properly free from the Greek doctrine about images. Its theologians have therefore had the difficult task of combining, on the question of images, as much as possible of the teaching of St. Thomas with doctrines formulated in a church which Roman Catholic historians such as Leclercq regard as having fallen, in this matter, into gross superstition.[1]

[1] À partir du Vme siècle, lorsque l'Église ne peut plus exercer sur les multitudes converties un contrôle suffisant, les emblèmes religieux se multiplient, se diversifient et nous avons montré dans un autre travail la croyance superstitieuse qui s'y attache dès lors fréquemment. La piété des fidèles ne distingue pas très habilement les objets dignes de sa vénération. Des légendes commencent à circuler, souvent puériles, quelquefois ridicules et qu'il faut se réjouir de rencontrer quand elles ne sont qu'inoffensives. Ainsi égarée, et souvent par des faussaires émérites, la piété confiante de nos pères se tourne vers des objets indignes d'elle, des représentations dépourvues de toute vérité historique. On ne conserve guère de mesure à l'égard de ces images que l'on confond avec celles qui représentent les mystères et les

Holy Images

On the crucial question whether an act of homage addressed to an image of Christ was an act of *latria* or not, Theodore took the opposite view to that of St. Thomas. When a view similar to that of St. Thomas was put before him—that such an act was an act of *latria*—he repelled it with vehemence. The utterances of Theodore on this subject, if they may be taken as representing the contemporary doctrine of the Greek Church, make that doctrine somewhat problematic. On the one hand, Theodore insists in some places, as strongly as it is possible to do, as strongly as St. Thomas does, that the homage offered to the image is the same as the homage offered to the person whom the image represents; on the other hand, he denies, as we have seen, that the homage offered to an image of Christ is an act of *latria*. He argues that it is impious to offer *latria* to any but the Holy Trinity. To offer homage to an image of Christ would be equivalent to asserting that the First and Third Persons of the Trinity had become incarnate as well as the Second. I can see no way of reconciling all these statements except on the supposition that Theodore held it wrong to offer *latria* to Christ Himself, apart from the other two Persons of the Trinity, to the Son, that is to say, incarnate. The image of Christ represents His human nature only. If so, we have in the doctrine of Theodore and the doctrine of Thomas two mutually contradictory doctrines, but each logically

---

scènes de la vie du Sauveur. L'exagération se manifeste également dans les témoignages rendus et le discrédit en rejaillit sur les images en général. Nul ne peut songer à nier les exagérations regrettables de la piété byzantine, souvent aussi choquante que la piété napolitaine dans l'expression de ses sentiments.

Dom H. Leclercq in the French translation of C. J. Hefele, *Histoire des Conciles*, tom. iii (2me Partie), p. 612.

St. Theodore of Studium

coherent in itself. They both agree in stating that the homage offered to the image of Christ is one and the same with the homage offered to Christ Himself, but then, since Theodore holds that it is wrong to offer *latria* to Christ by Himself, it follows that *latria* must not be offered to His image, whereas Thomas, holding that it is right to offer *latria* to Christ by Himself, maintains that it is right to offer *latria* to His image. The theology which later became predominant in the Roman Church seems to have combined a bit of Theodore's doctrine with a bit of Thomas's in unhappy self-contradiction. It asserts, with Thomas, that it is right to offer *latria* to Christ Himself, but asserts, with Theodore, that it is wrong to offer *latria* to His image.

But though by adopting elements of Greek theology, the Roman Church has been compelled to maintain that there *is* a kind of homage rendered to the images themselves, as distinct from the homage rendered to the persons whom the images represent: something of the caution which marked St. Gregory the Great and Charlemagne's bishops has held back the Roman Church from going the length of the Greeks. Images in the Latin West have never had the place in religion which wonder-working icons have had in Greek and Russian Christianity.[1]

The Roman Church does not go with St. John of Damascus in saying that the Second Commandment (or, as Rome reckons, the second part of the First Com-

---

[1] Of course, a distinction must be recognized between authoritative theology and popular practice. Even the local priesthood in some Catholic countries may encourage that superstition which it is their duty, according to the Tridentine Catechism, to guard against. I know of a recent case in Spain where an image was caused by a secret mechanism which the priest pressed with his foot to raise its arms, and the people were allowed to regard this as miraculous.

Holy Images

mandment) is abrogated for Christians. The whole Decalogue, according to the Tridentine Catechism, is obligatory for Christians. Only in regard to one Commandment—that relating to the Sabbath—it admits a certain difference. All the other Commandments of the Decalogue, the Catechism says, are natural and perpetual, and cannot for any reason be changed. True, the Law of Moses, as such, is abrogated, but all the Commandments comprised in the two tables are observed by Christians, not because they were commanded by Moses, but because they accord with nature. In the case of the Sabbath Commandment alone, the specification of the seventh day was something temporary and changeable: only the principle that a certain portion of time should be consecrated in each man's life to worship and the contemplation of divine things remains of obligation. This leaves us with the Commandment regarding the worship of images still obligatory in its original sense: St. John Damascene's way of escape is closed for us.

In regard to the honour to be offered to images, Roman doctrine seems to repudiate decisively the Greek view that a special *charis* and power resides in the image in consequence of the "overshadowing" of the Holy Spirit. The Decree of the Council of Trent lays it down that the images of Christ, of the Mother of God, and of the other saints are to be kept in churches and that the appropriate "honour and veneration" is to be shown them, but there must be no belief that any kind of divinity or power resides in them; no petition is to be addressed to them; no trust is to be set on them, such as the pagans of old time set upon their idols. The honour which is shown them passes through to the prototypes. Thus, when we kiss the images, when we uncover our heads

Doctrine of the Roman Church

before them and prostrate ourselves, that is only a means by which we worship (*adoramus*) Christ and venerate the saints whom the images represent.[1]

The Greek Church uses for the homage to be offered to the icons the word προσκυνεῖν which is a general term covering both the "worship" addressed to God and the homage offered to particular kinds of men. The Council of Trent avoided the term used of worship addressed to God (*adorare*) in speaking of the homage directed to images. In this way it conformed, verbally, with the ruling of St. Gregory the Great that images may be exhibited in churches, but must not be "adored." The homage directed to the image is only *veneratio*. This may not be satisfactory, since, as we have just seen, questionable consequences follow, if we suppose an inferior kind of homage to be addressed to the image distinct from the homage offered to the person represented. St. Thomas would have said that the gestures of homage directed to an image of Christ *were adoratio*, though he would presumably have refused to say that we adore the image: only the external gestures are directed to the image: the worship is addressed to Christ Himself.

But two different questions, it will be remembered, were involved in the controversy about images, not only the question whether it was right to address to them

[1] Imagines porro Christi, deiparae Virginis et aliorum sanctorum in templis praesertim habendas et retinendas, eisque debitum honorem et venerationem impertiendam, non quod credatur inesse aliqua in iis divinitas vel virtus, propter quam sint colendae, vel quod ab iis sit aliquid petendum, vel quod fiducia in imaginibus sit figenda, veluti olim fiebat a gentibus, quae in idolis spem suam collocabant: sed quoniam honos, qui eis exhibetur, refertur ad prototypa, quae illae repraesentant, ita ut per imagines, quas osculamur, et coram quibus caput aperimus et procumbimus, Christum adoremus, et sanctos quorum illae similitudinem gerunt, veneremur (Sessio XXV).

Holy Images

forms of homage, but the question whether it was right to make any plastic or pictorial representation of the Divine Being at all. On this question the practice of the Roman Church has differed from that of Eastern Christianity. Divine Majesty is affronted, the Tridentine Catechism says, by any attempt to represent the Divine Nature in material visible colours and shapes. You must not present anything which claims to be a portrait of God. That, of course, the Easterns had said too at the time of the Iconoclast controversy. And the Easterns had understood this to imply that you must not represent God the Father by any human shape. Such a conclusion the Roman Church did not draw. The Catechism of Trent lays it down that it is legitimate to represent God by the figure of an old man. There can be no real danger, it says, of anyone being so ignorant as to mistake such a picture for a portrait of God. It is a mere symbol indicating God's eternity and wisdom; an old man suggests length of life and is supposed (not always, unhappily, with truth) to imply wisdom. And it is interesting to note that the Catechism defends such a representation of God by a precisely similar argument to that by which Dio Chrysostom had defended, as we saw, a representation of Zeus. After all, Dio had said, Homer by a verbal description conjures up before your imagination a picture of Zeus, and, if that is permissible, it must be equally so to create a similar picture in your mind by a sculptured image. The Catechism appeals in the same way to the Book of Daniel. The description given in that book of the Ancient of Days, whose "garment was white as snow, and the hair of his head like the pure wool," calls up in our minds the visual image of an old man, who is understood to symbolize God. Thus, the

God Symbolized as an Old Man

Catechism infers, it is not impious to show the picture or image of an old man,[1] and say that it represents God, as long as it is clearly understood that it is a symbol, and not a portrait.

To-day one of the questions which was such a burning one in Constantinople eleven hundred years ago is no longer a matter of controversy. Protestants do not think it wrong to draw imaginary pictures of Jesus for the instruction of children and of the child-like. Few Protestants would consider Blake's illustrations to the Book of Job blasphemous, because they represent God by the figure of an old man. But the other question which troubled Christendom eleven hundred years ago is still a controversial one—whether it is right or wrong to address certain external gestures of homage to visible representations of Christ and of the saints now in the unseen world.

The question is different in regard to representations of Christ and in regard to representations of other persons in the unseen world; and for this reason. It is a fundamental Christian belief, common to all Christian churches, Catholic and Protestant, that Christ in the unseen world is in personal communication with those now on earth, that He is accessible to their prayers and active in bestowing good upon them. But Protestants deny that this is true of any other person in the unseen world. None of the saints can rightly be asked by those on earth to help them by their intercessions—whether because persons in the disembodied state are believed to be wholly unconscious, or to be unaware of passing events on earth, or to be inaccessible to the desires for

---

[1] The phrase translated "ancient of days" in Daniel means in the original simply "old man."

Holy Images

help which might be directed to them by individuals, or to be unable to help, or finally, because any attempt of the living to communicate with the dead seeks to overleap a barrier which God has ordained between the two worlds. While, therefore, it might be reasonable to direct marks of homage to a representation of Christ by an external gesture showing a movement of mind, in petition or thanksgiving or worship, towards Someone who really can have knowledge of such a movement, it might be unreasonable to direct marks of homage to a picture of St. John the Divine or of John Wesley.

With regard to gestures of homage addressed towards a representation of Christ, it is difficult to see how it can be regarded as of great moment what the external gesture is, if the movement of mind it expresses is right. Some members of the Society of Friends, I believe, have regarded it as superstitious to kneel in prayer, but Protestants generally regard this as proper. And, if it is right for anyone to address to Christ a desire for help or an inner act of devotion, it would not seem to call for censure, if he finds that he, for his part, can do this more intently when he has before him a picture of Christ or a crucifix—it being, of course, always understood that he does not regard the image as having any divine virtue residing in it or expect any help from it. So long as he regards the image as a mere material object which serves to call up certain thoughts and feelings in his mind when he looks at it, there can hardly be any ground for a charge of idolatry.

With regard to the representation of persons other than Christ, the question, as has just been said, must be different for Catholics and Protestants. But even to address some gestures of reverence to the picture or

Are Gestures of Homage Important?

statue of a great Christian, gone from this world, might seem harmless or appropriate to a Protestant, precisely as he takes off his hat when he passes the cenotaph. It does not happen to be the custom in Protestant circles to do this, and it does happen to be the custom for men to take off their hats when passing the cenotaph; but if any Wesleyan chose to take off his hat, or bow, whenever he passed a picture or statue of John Wesley, it might be thought a personal oddity; it would be hard to tax him with impiety or superstition. His act need not imply any particular belief about the mode of John Wesley's existence in the unseen world or the supposition that John Wesley is aware of the act of veneration: many people, no doubt, who salute the cenotaph, have no belief in any continued existence of the dead at all. It seems to them, nevertheless, appropriate to show by such a gesture that they remember the dead as worthy of honour.[1]

Suppose, then, the custom of venerating images which arose in the Church had meant no more than that statues or pictures of those who had played a heroic part

[1] This question regarding the precise nature of the homage rendered to a picture or statue may seem to many in England like theological hair-splitting remote from practical issues. There is, however, a part of the world to-day where such a question involves agonies of heart-searching and decision, with vast consequences for the life of the individual. Japanese Christians have to decide whether the gestures of homage which the Japanese Government requires everybody to render to the picture of the Emperor are religious in character, and have therefore to be refused, as idolatrous, by Christians, at the cost of all their worldly goods, or whether they are merely honorific, so that Japanese Christians need have no more scruple in rendering them than English Christians have in standing up when the King's picture is shown and *God Save the King* is sung at the conclusion of a cinema performance. Missionary opinion, I understand, is divided on the question.

Holy Images

in the life of the Church on earth were put up in places of worship, to recall what they did or said to the minds of the present generation, and that certain gestures were addressed to these images as an acknowledgment that those whom they represented were worthy of honour, there would not appear to be anything in such a custom to which Protestants, on their principles, need have objected. But, as a matter of fact, the custom of venerating images in Catholic Christianity has meant much more than this. It has meant the Catholic belief that saints in the unseen world could take knowledge of the desires of the living for their intercessions. The honours shown to the images, putting lighted candles before them, and so on, have expressed such desires directed to spirits who have passed into the Divine Presence. Here is a difference between Catholic and Protestant which matters. When, therefore, the controversy is represented as being concerned simply with the question whether it is right or wrong to address external homage of any kind to statues and pictures, it is misrepresented. There are some marks of veneration, as we have just seen, regarding which it is a matter of little moment whether they are addressed to the images of great men dead or not—a mere matter of custom or personal inclination. What really matters in the controversy is whether the Catholic belief about the continued fellowship between saints in the unseen world and those now on earth is true or not. It is only such marks of veneration as imply this belief which the Protestant is bound, on his presuppositions, to condemn. To act on that belief, even if a man addressed his cry for help to the saint in heaven without any image or picture or visible emblem at all, would, from the Protestant standpoint, be just as wrong as if his petition

A Difference which is Important

were accompanied by an external gesture directed to an image of the saint; whereas, on the other hand, if the Catholic belief is true, it matters little whether the saint is invoked with the eyes directed to a visible image or only by an inner movement. The question of the veneration of images is thus, by itself, a trivial one; the question of the Invocation of Saints is the important question behind the controversy, between Protestants on the one side and Roman Catholics and Orthodox on the other side, just as the question whether a divine virtue resides in the image or not is the important question on which Protestants and Roman Catholics agree against the Orthodox.

The Protestant objection to the use of images in worship is sometimes put in a form in which it is easy to refute, whereas the refutation does not meet a fundamental conviction in the Protestant mind. It is sometimes said by Protestants that the use of images in worship was a declension in the Christian Church after the first three centuries, because something material was introduced to help worship. A worship which dispensed with material aids, as Christian worship did at the outset, was necessarily more "spiritual."[1] But to such an objection the answer of the Catholic, already given by St. John of Damascus, that, so long as man is in the body, his religious life, like the rest of his life, must involve sense-stimulus from material things throughout, seems unquestionably valid. The higher life of the Spirit involves, on the Christian view of things, a use of, and domination

---

[1] This presupposition seems to underlie the article of W. Ellinger on the Iconoclastic Controversy contributed to *Forschungen zur Kirchengeschichte und zur christlichen Kunst* dedicated to Johannes Ficker on his seventieth birthday (Leipzig, 1931).

Holy Images

over, the material for the ends of the Spirit, but if we suppose a person cut off, not only from the impressions of sight and hearing, like Helen Keller, but from the impressions of smelling, tasting and touch as well, he would not thereby live a life of the purest spirituality. If worship were carried on in complete darkness, in which all visual impressions from the material surroundings were excluded, the worship would not thereby be more spiritual in a religious sense. The Protestant who states his objection in the way just noted is reminded that, even when he reads his Bible or hears a rousing sermon, his spiritual life is quickened by means of sense impressions from the material printed page or the vibrations of the material air, striking upon the bodily ear.

When, however, the Protestant objects to a false attribution of value to the material in religion, what is in his mind may, I think, be somewhat differently expressed, in a way which makes the Catholic answer just given wide of the mark. In the normal course of things any impression of sight or sound or any other sense affects our consciousness in a particular way; when we look at the printed page the words we read call up certain ideas, certain emotions, in our mind. That, so far, is just part of the common process of nature; nothing "supernatural" is involved. But now something else may follow belonging to the spiritual realm. The ideas, the emotions called up in my consciousness, accompanied by a particular direction of my will, may open my being to influences from the higher sphere, to the supernatural Grace of God. Protestants generally have no difficulty in believing that something more than the human person, something, in that sense, "supernatural," may come into operation in consequence of an inner act of faith or self-

The Material as a Vehicle

surrender. But they object to the supernatural being introduced into the first part of the process, the action of the sense-impression upon the consciousness: that must follow the wholly normal and natural mode by which certain material objects produce certain ideas and emotions in human minds. The words of Scripture may be spoken of as quickening my spiritual life by a supernatural Grace, but it is only when the printed text has first in the natural way produced a visible impression by which I apprehend, still in the natural way, a particular meaning. Upon my consciousness so conditioned, a supernatural Grace may fall, but the material object, the printed page, cannot directly procure the supernatural Grace; the effect cannot be short-circuited without my consciousness, conditioned in a particular way, coming in as intermediary.

This will be seen if we take the Catholic doctrine of Baptismal Regeneration. When the Protestant objects to this, in the case of a baby, it is because the spiritual effect is held to be produced directly, by the sprinkling of water upon the baby's body, without the requisite conditioning of the baby's consciousness. A Protestant would not necessarily object to the belief that Regeneration was effected, say in a grown-up convert to Christianity who received Baptism. All the sense impressions bearing upon the convert at that supreme moment, the sound of the words read, perhaps the tune of the hymns, the feeling of being immersed or sprinkled, might help to condition his consciousness in a particular way, upon which the beginning of a new life might ensue. Thus the ordinary argument defending Catholic sacramental belief, that you cannot eliminate from religion the part played by material things in stimulating the senses, will

Holy Images

be seen to be quite wide of the mark when urged against the Protestant objection stated as it has just been stated. We may be ready to allow any amount of sense-stimulation in religion, and not abandon Protestant principles, so long as the material object is not held to produce the supernatural effect directly, but only to condition consciousness in the way it normally would. It is the view that the effect may be produced directly by the material object or the external gesture which is repudiated by the Protestant as "magic." There may be a valid answer from the Catholic side, but it should be clear that the ordinary argument will not serve.

When we now apply these considerations to the use of images and pictures in worship, we see that the crucial question is whether any power is held to reside in the image by which it can produce an effect, let it be an inward spiritual grace or bodily healing or the averting of some danger, otherwise than by calling up certain ideas and feelings by a natural process in the minds of persons who look at it. There are Protestants who believe that bodily disease can be cured by an act of faith in the Divine Healer. If so, it would seem unreasonable to deny that a picture of Christ laying His hand upon the sick might conceivably make the apprehension of His present power more vivid, and so help to generate the act of faith, upon which healing follows. But if you suppose that a wooden board upon which a figure of Christ is painted might, if brought into contact with the sick body, cure the disease directly without first conditioning the sick man's consciousness in the normal way in which a picture should, that, from the Protestant standpoint, is superstition. Yes, there are those handkerchiefs brought from the body of St. Paul, that shadow

What Protestants Think Superstitious

of St. Peter, which will never cease to be brought up against the Protestant in this connexion. Frankly, it would be easier for the Protestant if they were not there. Perhaps, in the end, he has got either to throw over St. Luke or qualify his conviction that no supernatural power can ever, in any circumstances, reside in a material object. And then he is faced with the problem: if it ever can, what are the circumstances which make it possible? An intricate and troublesome inquiry! Many modern Protestants do not have much compunction in choosing the simpler alternative, throwing over St. Luke at this point.

The upshot of our argument so far is that, provided no belief is entertained of a supernatural power residing in images, the use of images and pictures in religion to call up particular recollections, ideas, emotions, is, even from the Protestant standpoint, harmless. But a further question may be raised. Granting that such a use of pictures is permissible for those who believe themselves spiritually helped in that way, is it likely that images and pictures do, as a matter of fact, give any help of a distinctively religious kind?

To symbolize God by the figure of an old man, says the Tridentine Catechism, is harmless because no one could take the image for more than a symbol. The old man depicted suggests wisdom, and so you may be led by looking at the picture to think more vividly of God as wise. The trouble is that the picture of an old man does not suggest wisdom in the abstract: it suggests wisdom only as a constituent in a particular individual person, an individual wisdom which is not quite the same as the wisdom which is the constituent of another individual person. No representation of a human form, especially no representation of a human face, however

Holy Images

rudely drawn, but has a particular individual expression, and every individual expression suggests to us a whole personality behind it. How it is that we read a particular character straight off from the features of a human face may be mysterious; we cannot, of course—unless we have some abnormal gift—read the character in such a way that we could state with any certainty what qualities, described in general terms, belong to it; we may be quite mistaken as to whether the person is good or bad, agreeable or disagreeable; but there is a certain fundamental individuality which any face by itself suggests—the faces of complete strangers, for instance, which we see round us in a railway compartment. You cannot present the picture of any human face to our eyes without immediately suggesting to our minds a particular personality to which that face, and that face alone, could belong. The picture of an old man, symbolizing God, is thus not the picture of "Old Man" in the abstract, but the picture of one particular old man, the existent or non-existent old man whom our imagination inevitably and immediately conjures up or creates on sight of the picture. It is a particular human personality with which you occupy my mind when I want to think about God. And if it is the qualities of wisdom or dignity or benevolence the picture is meant to suggest, it gives all those qualities, if it does successfully suggest them, stamped with so individual a note that it makes it harder for me, not easier, to think of God's wisdom or dignity or benevolence apart from the wisdom, dignity, and benevolence of a particular imagined old man. And to attribute to God the wisdom, dignity, and benevolence of this particular old man is, it need not be said, unworthy of God. It is not because the picture is material that it is unworthy,

A False Personality Interposed

but because it interposes an alien personality. If we were really going to think of God as like any old man whom any artist has ever drawn, the unworthiness of the representation would certainly reach the degree of blasphemy. If we look with pleasure at Blake's illustrations to the Book of Job and do not feel them blasphemous, it is because it never occurs to us to treat them as aids to religion at all: we look at them purely from the artistic, not from the religious, point of view. Probably no one, in praying to God, has ever tried to direct his mind to the old man drawn by Blake.

The representation of Christ and Christian saints is on a different footing from symbols of God, inasmuch as Christ and the saints wore a visible human form when they were on earth. The controversy between Iconoclasts and Orthodox regarding images of Christ seems to us now a beating of the air. As against the Iconoclast contention that Christ, as God, was essentially unrepresentable by any picture or image, the Orthodox asserted with perfect justice that Christ had a real human body and therefore a body with contours and colours which an artist could represent. But this was quite inadequate as justification of the Orthodox and Catholic practice. The question is not whether Christ had a body which an artist, had he been there, could have drawn: the question is whether pictures of Christ drawn now, according to an artist's fancy, without any knowledge what He really looked like, are helpful to devotion.

And here the Iconoclast argument which, as it stands, seems nonsense, may be trying to say something true—the argument that by showing a circumscribed (περίγραπτος, outlined) figure as Christ, you are in effect trying to add a fourth Person to the Holy Trinity.

Holy Images

For, as we saw just now, every human figure, at any rate every human face, presents us with a kind of notation from which we immediately read off a particular individual personality. The person the picture shows has his own peculiar individuality and (unless by some incredible fluke an artist were to hit off a precise likeness of Jesus without knowing it) it is a different individuality from that of Jesus. My thought of Jesus is thus confused by the intrusion of another quite different person. If I direct my thought, or my prayers, to a fancy picture of Jesus, it is impossible for my idea of Jesus to be uncontaminated by the alien personality.

This evil in the case of pictures of Jesus has, no doubt, to some extent been corrected by the very multitude of pictures, differing as they do one from another. That has to some extent restored to us a liberating vagueness of outline—as in the case of a composite photograph made by superimposing a number of different photographed faces one upon the other—which may obviate our imagination being too much held by the accidents of one particular picture. Most of us, I suppose, have a more or less floating picture of Jesus in our minds made up of all the thousands of pictures we have seen since childhood. Yet it must be remembered that nearly all these pictures conform to a certain type which was quite possibly not that of the real Jesus—the bearded face, with the hair parted in the middle and falling down in long locks on either side upon the shoulders. Some of the early representations of Jesus, in painting or bas-relief, show Him, as we saw, beardless with comparatively short hair. There is no reason to believe that either type rests on any authentic tradition. Both are early works of fancy. There is some greater probability in the bearded

What did Jesus Look Like?

type, since it is unlikely that the custom of shaving clean had found much entry among the Jews of Palestine. In regard to the long hair, it may be that the Iconoclasts were right when they asserted that this had been given in the first instance to Jesus, because He was supposed to have been a Nazarite, from a confusion of "Nazarite" with "Nazarene."[1] "Nazarite" was the name given in the Mosaic Law to a man who undertook a vow to abstain from all intoxicating drink and let his hair grow long. We know that Jesus drank wine, and cannot therefore have been a Nazarite. In any case the picture which we all have in our imaginations of Jesus is a fancy picture. It would probably be a severe shock to us now, if we could see Jesus as He really was on earth, and found that the familiar type was quite unlike the reality. It would cause us acute mental discomfort to fit the new personality discovered to the Jesus we have had in our minds since childhood; we should find ourselves saying again and again. Can this stranger with the unfamiliar appearance really be Jesus?[2]

What has been said regarding representations of Jesus applies in its measure to pictures and images of the early saints. Can I get more real grasp of St. Paul's personality, can I direct my desires more effectively, if, as Catholics believe, St. Paul in the unseen world can receive the

[1] Κόμην γὰρ ἔχοντα τὸν Σωτῆρα γράφουσιν ἐξ ὑπονοιᾶς διὰ τὸ Ναζωραῖον αὐτὸν καλεῖσθαι, ἐπείπερ οἱ Ναζιραῖοι κόμας ἔχουσιν. Σφάλλονται δὲ οἱ τοὺς τύπους αὐτῷ συνάπτειν πειρώμενοι· οἶνον γὰρ ἔπινεν ὁ Σωτήρ, ὃν οἱ Ναζιραῖοι οὐκ ἔπινον—Nicephorus adv. Epiph. xix. 81 (K. Holl, Frag. 24).

[2] A crucifix is perhaps less open to the objection here urged than any other plastic representation of Jesus, because the face (except in very large crucifixes) is less distinctly seen, and the figure upon the cross can therefore stand for the Man, less marked with individual characteristics.

Holy Images

thoughts and desires I address to him, when I have before me the picture of someone else, whom an artist's fancy has substituted for Paul? I think we may allow that where we have real knowledge what someone in the past looked like, where we have a good painting of him or a photograph, it may be a great help to look at it when we try to apprehend the person in question. But supposing, by ignorance, someone made a confusion. Supposing he mistook, let us say, a photograph of Cardinal Manning for a photograph of Cardinal Newman, and in all that he read and heard about Cardinal Newman, pictured him according to the photograph of Manning, could we say that the photograph had been a great help to him in getting hold of Newman's personality? Manning was probably much more like Newman than most of the persons shown in pictures to represent St. Paul are like St. Paul.

In answer to such an argument it may be said that inevitably we form a visual image in our minds of any person about whom we are told, and where it is quite impossible to know what the person really looked like, the idea of him formed by an artist may be a better one for me to contemplate than any my own mind would form unaided. Now it has, I believe, been established by modern psychology that the extent and distinctness with which people form visual images of the things about which they are told, differs enormously from one individual to another. Some people, it is said, form practically no visual images. In the case of the great majority the visual images they do form are fluctuating and blurred. Unquestionably a painted picture of St. Paul, if anyone directs his mind to it as a real likeness of St. Paul, gives him a much sharper and steadier mental image

Vaguer and Clearer Visualization

than he would have if he merely for himself visualized St. Paul internally from the expressions of St. Paul's personality in his written words. Unfortunately it does so by substituting another personality for St. Paul. True, without the picture the student of St. Paul would probably have some visual image of St. Paul, which (except in the event of an incredible fluke) would be a wrong one. But its relative vagueness would give it less hold on his mind than the personality shown in a picture. A person who read Cardinal Newman's life without ever seeing either a portrait of Newman or a portrait he mistook for Newman's, would no doubt form a visual image of him unlike the real Newman. But if in the end he were shown a portrait of Newman the relatively vague image he had had in his mind would dissolve easily and allow itself to be superseded by the image of the real Newman without trouble. If on the other hand he had had a clear mental picture all the time derived from a portrait of Manning, the conflict between the two images, when he saw a portrait of Newman, would be mentally uncomfortable. The vagueness of the unassisted visual image, its being so much less binding, would prove to have been an advantage.

It may be said that, although the picture or image no doubt substitutes a different personality, and so adulterates the idea of a person drawn otherwise from true verbal statements about him or his preserved words, this disadvantage is more than compensated for by its giving the idea of the person, in other respects true, greater force, greater hold upon the thoughts and affections. In the case of persons of significance for religion the important thing is that this force and hold upon the thoughts and affections should be as great as possible. If the

Holy Images

picture helps to secure this, its relative falsehood does not much matter. This seems to me to imply a presupposition very questionable in psychology—that an idea exercises power upon us in ratio to the distinctness of the visual image which we form in connexion with it. So far from this being true, it is very often the vague and indistinct suggestiveness which gives an idea power. A person who has a very wavering indistinct visual image of St. Paul, who, if questioned, could hardly say whether he thinks of him as black-haired or white-haired or bald, may have a more vivid sense of St. Paul's personality and be more moved by it, than someone who has as distinct a visual image of St. Paul as he has of someone whom he actually knows in life. It would be absurd to suppose that those who believe in a personal God have a greater or less sense of His presence according as they attach a more or less distinct visual image to the thought of Him.

These considerations would point to the conclusion that the specifically religious use of pictures and images, simply as means to make more vivid to our apprehension a person in the unseen world and stimulate devotion, is very small indeed. Most people to-day would feel that pictures and images are religiously indifferent: they would neither share the Iconoclastic passion against them as idolatrous nor the Orthodox passion for them as an essential element in the Christian cult. We value pictures on grounds quite other than the specifically religious, as giving us an aesthetic pleasure, when they are good art, not as giving us religious uplift. If Anglicans like to have their places of worship decorated with sacred pictures, figures of Christ and Prophets and Apostles in the stained-glass windows, it will be simply because

Why Images are Valued

the consciousness of rich adornment round them, adornment which is aesthetically pleasing, attunes their frame of mind sympathetically, as the beauty of music does, to acts of worship, not that the figures on the walls or in the windows, taken individually, give them any fresh sense of the personalities represented. Of course, in many churches it is rather aesthetic discomfort than aesthetic pleasure which one gets from modern painted figures and modern stained glass, though in this case the psychological law which makes us cease to be conscious of what is familiar may work beneficently.

If in the past the question of images in religion has excited such passion, for and against, that is certainly because they were not thought of as simply means to bring home to the mind of the worshipper an unseen person, but because the other view of them, as means to act upon the unseen person, or as themselves charged with a quasi-personal supernatural power, was always there in the background. Apart from that there was no reason why it should not have been left entirely to each individual's discretion to use pictures and images or not, according as he found them helpful or not helpful. In such a matter it is plain that the attempt to enforce one rule for everybody would take no account of the great varieties of individual temperament and mode of suggestibility. But the rage and indignation of the Orthodox against those who would do dishonour to the images shows that they thought of the images as much more than a mere means of suggestion. The images themselves claimed honour in the way which only persons properly do. Their champions felt that a slight was being offered to beings in whose cause the extreme of ardour and self-devotion was called for. This multitude of icons had

Holy Images

come to be a people of protectors and helpers dwelling in the churches, surrounding and watching over the Christian people still in the flesh, themselves, as it were, part of the Christian family, without whom the company of those still struggling in the world would be forlorn. There was, one gathers, a joy and surge of affection raised by the visible presence of this army of older members of the family who had been victorious and passed on.

If such an attitude to the images, such a feeling towards them, as if they were in some sense animate, was a delusion, if the result was deplorable superstition, it may still be asked whether the delusion did not come in to fill a certain gap, which Protestantism has perhaps not filled quite satisfactorily. Image-worship in the eighth century did mean a vivid thought of the great company of those who had passed into the unseen as still in effective solidarity with the Church on earth. It was a Methodist-Anglican poet who wrote:

> "One family, we dwell in Him,
> One Church, above, beneath,
> Though now divided by the stream,
> The narrow stream of death.
>
> One army of the Living God,
> To His command we bow;
> Part of His host have crossed the flood,
> And part are crossing now."

But if this is true, it may be thought that in Protestant forms of worship, that truth has never been brought home by visible symbols as it is brought home by the array of pictures or images, representing those who have gone on before, in the worship of Catholic Christianity, East and West.

INDEX

Abbaye, Rabbi, 53, 54
Abgar, prince of Edessa, 145
Abodah Zarah, 51, 53¹, 60¹, 61, 63 (62²)
Abraham, worships the sons of Heth, 141; pictures of Abraham and Isaac, 58, 119
Abydos in Egypt, 23
Acheiropoieta, 145
Acts, Book of the, 78; see also "St. Luke"
Adonis, 35, 75
Aeschylus, 28
Africa, negroes of west coast, 32
Aion, Greek god, 35
Alba, city in Italy, 26
Alexander the Great, 25, 28, 93, 103
Alexandria, 122
Alexandrine Fathers, 34, 35; see also "Clement of Alexandria," "Origen"
Alviella, Count G. de, 32¹
Amen-Ra, Egyptian god, 25
Aniconic objects of veneration, 13–16, 41–43
Ansaldi, C. J., 148²
Anticlides, 32
Antisthenes the Cynic, 65
Antony, Mark, 26
Aphrodite, image of, 60; see also "Venus"
Apollo, 22, 26, 99
Argos, 24
Aristonicus of Pergamon, 25
Aristophanes, Scholia on, 29¹, 32
Aristotle, quoted, 150; statues of, 104

Arnobius, 15¹
Artemis, image of, at Ephesus, 78; image of, at Alexandria, 79
Arya Somaj, the, 36
Ascalon, 60
Ascoli, synagogue at, 62
Asherim, 41
Asklepios, 112; the Hermetic tract, *Asklepios*, 24, 25, 33, 34
Asterius, bishop of Amasea, 109
Athanasius, Saint, 122
Athena (Pallas), 15, 22, 23–25; A. Skiras, 29
Athenaeus, 25², 30¹, 32
Athenagoras, 52³, 93, 94
Athens, 25, 27–30
Attis, 75
Augustine, Saint, 26, 66, 67¹, 119–124, 137
Azriel Trabot, Rabbi, 62

Babylonians, the, 28
Baptismal Regeneration, 167
Barlaam, martyr, 118
Barnabas, Epistle of, 98
Baruch, Book of, 19
Basil, Saint, 118, 130, 142
Bethel, worship of the Calf at, 43
Beyer and Lietzmann, 56²
Bidez, J., 74¹
Blake, William, 161, 171
Boaz, Isaiah, 62²
Borries, Bodo de, 67¹
Bréhier, Emile, 76¹
Buddhist art, early, 102, 103
Butades of Sicyon, 52

Caesar, Julius, 25

179

Callimachus, 15¹, 24
Caroline Books, the, 147
Carpocratians, the, 104, 105
Celsus, 92
Charis (Grace), 144, 158
Charlemagne, the Emperor, 147
Cherub, Cherubim, 49, 54, 55, 87, 133, 134
Chesterton, G. K., 112
Cicero, 67, 68
Clement of Alexandria, 22¹, 65, 66, 86, 87, 94, 107
Clerc, Charly, 26
Commandment, the Second, 44–49, 85–87, 104, 106, 107, 110, 132, 133, 157
Constantia, sister of the Emperor Constantine, 110–112
Constantine I, the Emperor, 98, 99, 112, 114, 118
Constantine V, the Emperor, 135
Corinthians, First Epistle to the, 90
Coriolanus, 33
Crooke, W., 31¹
Cross, the, 98, 99, 109, 118, 140, 141
Crucifix, the, 113, 173²
Crucifixion, depicted, 97–99
Curtius Rufus, 28¹
Cynics, the, 65

Daemons, 91–94
Damascius, 34, 35
Daniel, Book of, 160, 161
David, 43
Dayananda Saraswati, Swami, 36
Decalogue, the, 44, 46, 136–138, 158
Delattre, P., 57
Delphi, 26
Demeter, 75
Demetrius, Macedonian prince, 30

Deuteronomy, Book of, 40, 90, 134
Devils, 90–92
Didascalia, Egyptian, 86
Dio Cassius, 25, 33
Dio Chrysostom, 64, 70–75, 160
Diogenes the Cynic, of Sinope, 65
Diogenes Laertius, 22⁴
Dionysius of Halicarnassus, 33
Dionysius II, of Syracuse, 21, 22
Dionysus, 75
Dioscuri, aniconic representation of, 15
Dura-Europus, Synagogue at, 57–59, 67
Durandus, 150
Dvornik, Professor F., 148

Egypt, 23–25, 33–35
Elijah, 68
Elisha, 42, 143
Elliger, W., 56²⁻³, 84¹, 97¹, 117¹, 165¹
Elmslie, W. A. L., 51
Elvira, Synod of, 114–116, 120, 141¹
Ephesus, 78
Epicureans, the, 72
Epiphanius, Deacon, 154
Epiphanius, Saint, 51–53, 117
Erman, A., 23, 24
Eros, images of, at Thespiae, 15
Eugenius, Pope, 148
Euhemerus, 93
Eusebius, 98¹, 110–112
Exodus, Book of, 42⁴, 49
Ezekiel, 58; Book of, 54, 55

Fetish-worship, 13, 14, 32, 37
Fortuna Muliebris, image of, 33
Foucher, A., 102
Frankfort, Council of, 147
Frazer, Sir James, 15⁵, 28

Index

Frey, J. B., 56[1, 2], 57[2]
Friends, Society of, 162
Funk, F. X., 114

Galilee, synagogues in, 57, 59
Gamaliel II, Rabbi, 49, 60
Gamast, Jewish sepulchral chambers at, 57
Gandhara school of sculpture, 103
Gardner, Professor Percy, 84
Garrucci, R., 4, 56[1]
God the Father, represented by symbol of old man, 119, 160, 161, 169, 170
Grace, *see* Charis
Graziano, Italian Rabbi, 62
Gregory, Saint, of Nyssa, 118
Gregory of Tours, 99
Gregory I, Pope, 125–127, 131, 147, 148, 159
Gregory II, Pope, 154
Gregory III, Pope, 146
Grumel, V., 153

Hadrian I, Pope, 146, 148
Hamman Lif, synagogue at, 57
Harnack, A., 115
Hasmonaean dynasty, the, 48
Hayyôth, the, 54, 55
Hector of Troy, 26
Heinemann, I., 67–70
Hera, 15, 20, 25
Heraclitus, 64, 65
Heraïskos, 34, 35
Hermas, 105
Hermes, 15, 21, 75, 100
Hermetic literature, 24; *see* "Asklepios"
Herod Antipas, 48
Hezekiah, king, 43
Hiero, Sicilian tyrant, 26
Hinduism, 16, 31, 35, 37
Holl, Karl, 117[1]

Homer, 73
Horace, 21, 30, 31
Horus, Egyptian god, 23
Hosea, Book of, 40

Iamblichus, 77
Ilion, 26
Invocation of Saints, the, 161, 162, 164, 165
Irenaeus, Saint, 104, 105
Isaac al Fasi, 62[2]
Isaiah, Book of, 18, 28
Ishmael, Rabbi, 49
Isidore of Pelusium, 79
Islam, *see* "Mohammedanism"
Italy, south, 20, 21, 157[1]

Jacob, 140
Japanese Christians, 163
Jehovah, 40, 44, 46, 54, 58
Jeremy, Epistle of, 19
Jerusalem, 48
Jesus, representations of in painting and sculpture, 97–102, 104, 110–112, 118–120, 124, 134, 135, 161, 171–173
Job, Book of, Blake's illustrations to, 161, 171
John Chrysostom, Saint, 118
John of Damascus, Saint, 128–144, 157, 158, 165
Joseph and his brethren, 140
Josephus, 48
Joshua, Book of, 131, 140
Joshua ben Levi, Rabbi, 83
Jupiter of the Capitol, 22
Justin Martyr, Saint, 94, 98, 106[1]

Kaufmann, Carl Maria, 96
Kaufmann, D., 62
Keller, Helen, 166
King-worship, Hellenistic, 69
Kings, Second Book of, 42[2, 3]

181

Holy Images

Knoepfler, A., 104, 105[1]
Koch, Hugo, 84[1], 105[1], 109[2], 111[1], 124
Kohl, H., and C. Watzinger, 57, 59[2]
Kore (Persephone), 75
Kraeling, C. H.

Lachares, 22
Lactantius, 68
Lagarde, A. P. de, 86[3]
Lagrange, M. J., 44
Lajpat Rai, Lala, 36
Lane E. W., 81[1]
Lateran Council, the, 146
Latria, 138, 150–152, 156, 157
Leclercq, H., 57[1, 2], 114[1], 155
Leo III, the Emperor, 128, 135, 154
Leontius of Neapolis, Bishop, 129
Leviticus, Book of, 61, 90
Lewis the Pious, Western Emperor, 145, 147
Lions, carved, in synagogues, 62, 63; used medically, 62[2]
Loewe, Professor H., 53[1], 61, 106[1]
Lucian, 15[1], 21, 27
Lucilius, 22
Lucullus, 33
Luke, Saint, 86, 144, 169

Magic, sympathetic, 27, 28
Maimonides, 50
Mani, Manichaeans, 111, 119, 141
Martin, E. J., 128[1]
Martin, Saint, 125
Maspéro, G., 25
Maximus of Tyre, 64, 70, 71
Mecca, black stone of, 43
Melkarth, Phoenician god, 28
Merton College at Oxford, 53[1]
Michael II, the Emperor, 145, 148
Migné in France, 98[1]

Minucius Felix, 32, 68, 93
Mohammedanism, 16, 43, 80–82, 87, 133
Monophysites, the, 134, 135
Moses, 40, 43, 44, 46, 58, 67, 70, 87, 106, 107, 141, 142, 158
Mother, the Great, 78
Mummius, 33

Nahum ben Simai, 60, 61
Nehardea, synagogue at, 61
Neoplatonism, 75–77, 91
Neryllinus, 94
Nestorians, the, 135
New Zealand natives, 32
Nicaea, Second Council of, 129, 146, 153–155; repudiated by Charlemagne, 147
Nicephorus, Patriarch of Constantinople, 130, 173[1]
Nike (Victory), image of, 25, 61, 74
Nilus, 127
Norden, E., 144[1]

Octavian, 26
Old Testament, 17–19, 39–45, 58, 87, 90, 129, 132, 133, 140
Olympia, images at, 27, 73
Ophannim ("Wheels"), 49
Origen, 86–89, 107
Orpheus, 100
Osiris, 35
Ostrogorsky, G., 117[1], 148[1]
Otto, Rudolf, 36, 37

Palaeolithic drawings, 14
Panion, statue at, 112
Paschal I, Pope, 146
Paul, Saint, 71, 90, 91, 110, 118, 120, 137, 138, 143, 169
Paulinus of Nola, 124–126
Pausanias, 15[3], 27, 28

182

Index

Pergamon, 25
Persian art, Mohammedan, 81, 82
Pesaro, synagogue at, 79
Peter, Saint, 143, 169
Pharae in Achaia, 15
Phidias, 16, 22, 23, 73
Philo of Alexandria, 70
Philostratus, 26, 27
Pilate, Pontius, 48
Plato, Platonism, 82, 87, 88, 91, 104, 123
Pliny the Elder, 52[3]
Plotinus, 75, 76
Plutarch, 15[4], 22, 26, 33, 66, 91
Polydamas, athlete, 27
Porphyry, 74, 91, 108
Posidonius, 66–68, 70
Praxiteles, 15, 16
Priapus, 21, 75
Protesilaus, 27
Psalms quoted, 18, 40, 90, 140
Pseudo-Clementine Church Order, 86
Ptolemy, king of Egypt, 79
Pythagoras, 104, 107

Rabbinic doctrine, 49–63, 69, 83, 106[1]
Reinach, Théodore, 67[2]
Reitzenstein, R., 35[1], 67
Rhea, 75
Rome, catacombs in, 55, 56, 97–101; image transported from Pessinus, 79
Romulus, 66
Rostovtseff, M., 58

Samos, Samians, 15, 20
Samuel, Second Book of, 42[1]
Samuel, Rabbi, 54
Sassanian king, 61
Schürer, Emil, 55

Scott, Walter (editor of *Hermetica*), 24
Seneca, 68, 78[1]
Serenus of Marseilles, Bishop, 125, 126
Serpent, the brazen, 43, 106, 133
Serug, 51, 52
Shepherd, the Good, 100, 105, 110, 112
Shesheth, Rab, 49
Shiltē hag-Gibbōrīm, 62[2]
Shiva, 36
Simon Magus, 111
Sinai, Mount, 42
Siwa, Oasis of, 25
Skira, festival of, at Athens, 29
Solomon ibn Adret, 62[2]
Solomon, King, 133
Spain, 114, 115, 157[1]
Spiritualism, 94
Star-worship, 69, 70
Stephen II and Stephen III, Popes, 146
Stilpo, 22, 23
Stoics, the, 65, 72–75
Stone Age, the Early, 14
Strabo, 67, 70
Strack, H. L., and P Billerbeck, 60
Suidas, 34, 35
Sukenik, E. L., 59[2]
Sulpicius Severus, 125
Sybaris, 25

Tabernacle, the, 48
Tarasius, 154
Tarquinius Priscus, 66
Tatian, 89, 93
Temple, the, 49, 140
Terah, 52
Tertullian, 85, 86, 88, 96, 105–107, 112
Theagenes of Thasos, 27

Holy Images

Themis, 75
Theodore of Studium, 142[1], 145, 153, 156, 157
Theophilus, Byzantine Emperor, 128
Thespiae, images of Eros at, 15
Thomas Aquinas, Saint, 150–153, 155–157
Thrace, Thracian Chersonese, 27
Thurston, the Rev. H., 99 (98[1])
Tiberias, 48
Tixeront, J., 114, 115
Toxaris, 27
Trajan, the Emperor, 51
Tralles, 25
Trent, Council of; Tridentine Catechism, 130, 157[1], 158–160, 169
Trinity, the Holy, 119, 156, 171
Tyre, 28

Uzzah. 48

Varro, 66
Venus, 30, 31
Victory, see "Nike"
Virgin Mary, the Blessed, 101, 144, 153, 158
Vishnu, 37

Watzinger, C., 57, 59
Wesley, Charles, 178; John, 162, 163
Wisdom, Book of, 18, 19, 68, 69
Wolff, G., 32[2]
Wulff, O., 59[1]

Xenophanes, 65

Zacharias, Pope, 146
Zeno of Citium, 65, 78
Zeus, 21, (Ktesios) 32, 61, 73, 74
Zoroastrianism, 16

For Product Safety Concerns and Information please contact our EU
representative GPSR@taylorandfrancis.com
Taylor & Francis Verlag GmbH, Kaufingerstraße 24, 80331 München, Germany

www.ingramcontent.com/pod-product-compliance
Lightning Source LLC
Chambersburg PA
CBHW060348190426
43201CB00043B/1760